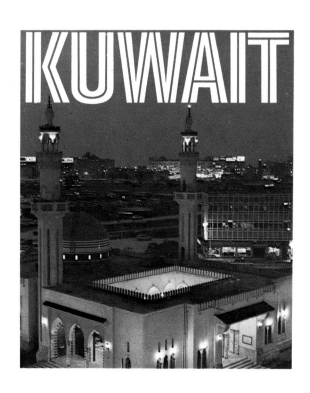

KUWAIT

كويت

RALPH SHAW

M

Title page:
His Highness the
Amir Shaikh Sabah
as-Salim as-Sabah

Front jacket: The tourist towers
on the Corniche, in Kuwait
City. Back jacket: Water-
towers assure an adequate
supply of water as well as
providing a striking example of
modern Kuwaiti architecture.
Half-title page: A part of
Kuwait City at night with the
Telecommunications Centre in
the background and a Mosque
in the foreground.   Opposite:
The Telecommunications Centre
in Kuwait City.

© Ministry of Information,
Kuwait, 1976

Compiled under the auspices of
Mass Consultants and Services,
Kuwait

Design by David Warner
Augustine Studios

First published 1976 by
Macmillan London Limited
London and Basingstoke
Associated companies in
New York, Toronto, Dublin,
Melbourne, Johannesburg
and Delhi

Filmset by Servis Filmsetting
Ltd. Manchester
Printed and bound in Great
Britain by Chromoworks Ltd.
Nottingham and
Chapel River Press, Andover

British Library Cataloguing
in Publication Data
Shaw, Ralph
   Kuwait,
   Index.
   ISBN 0-333-21247-9
   953'.67'05 DS 2   47.K8
   Kuwait

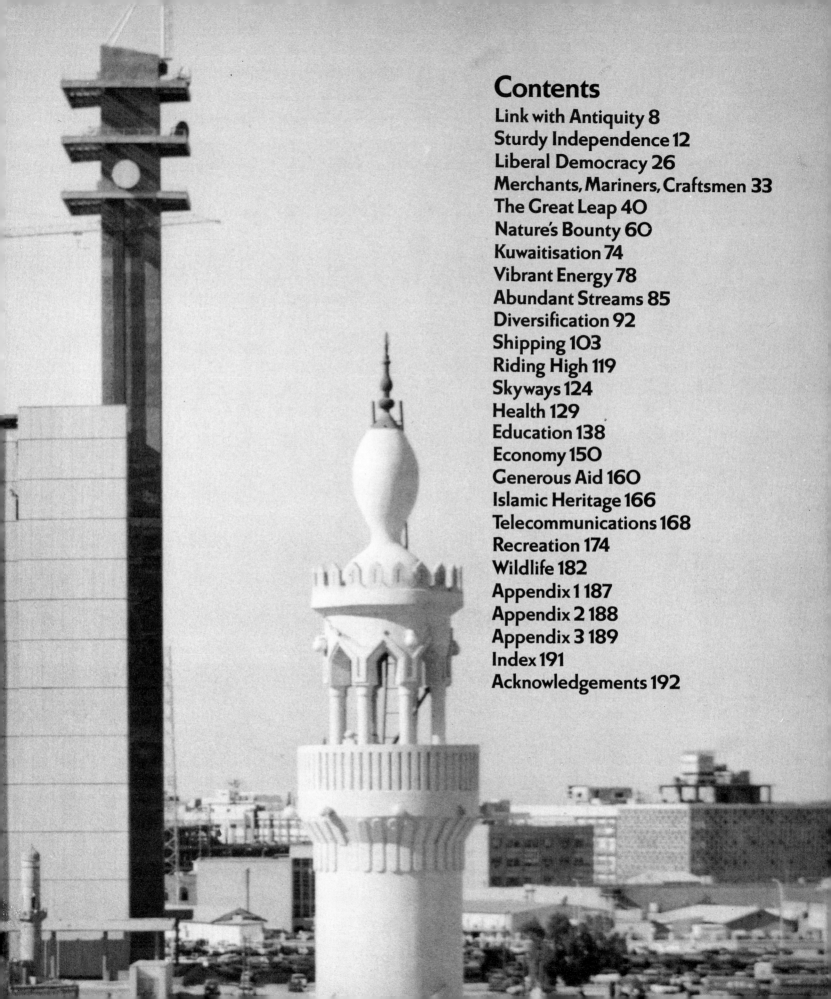

Contents

Link with Antiquity 8
Sturdy Independence 12
Liberal Democracy 26
Merchants, Mariners, Craftsmen 33
The Great Leap 40
Nature's Bounty 60
Kuwaitisation 74
Vibrant Energy 78
Abundant Streams 85
Diversification 92
Shipping 103
Riding High 119
Skyways 124
Health 129
Education 138
Economy 150
Generous Aid 160
Islamic Heritage 166
Telecommunications 168
Recreation 174
Wildlife 182
Appendix 1 187
Appendix 2 188
Appendix 3 189
Index 191
Acknowledgements 192

Kuwait

Link
with Antiquity

The name of Kuwait today is synonymous with oil and the international power the State's prosperity has bestowed on the country and its people in an industrialised world dependent on crude oil as the main source of energy. Kuwait today ranks among the most modern and progressive communities in the world and yet its emergence from regional obscurity has been accomplished at a phenomenal speed compared with the time-spans of development elsewhere. History—judged by the contrast between old and new—goes back no more than twenty-five years, the time when the national heritage, dating distantly and with little evolutionary change to the early eighteenth century, was completely transformed by the underground reservoirs of oil discovered under the sands. Further back still there lies the fascination of the region's ancient history, its archaeological treasure-chest of links with the lost civilisation of Dilmun and other areas of antiquity.

The focal point of this exploration of the relics of an ancient past is the small island of Failaka at the entrance to Kuwait Bay. It has provided an abundance of clues which may throw light on the ancient civilisations of the world, the great nations and the peoples whose existence is shrouded in the dimness of the remote ages of Mankind. In 1958, a Danish archaeological expedition discovered the first Bronze Age finds at Failaka. Earlier, the expedition had shed new light on the location of the lost community of Dilmun by excavations at Bahrain. Many archaeologists now believe that the Gulf region was part, if not the whole, of an early civilisation contemporary with those of Mesopotamia and India.

The excavations at Failaka—easier than those at Bahrain—unearthed valuable evidence of Kuwait's ancient history and the region's links with the earliest emergence of civilisation. They offered sound evidence that Failaka and Bahrain had been in contemporary association. This was the link with Dilmun, a civilisation dated about 2800 BC, the period of Gilgamesh. All the pieces of the archaeological jigsaw have not yet been found but the evidence points clearly to Failaka's existence for 4,000 years or more as a holy island, at one time probably an outpost of Dilmun located 250 miles away on Bahrain Island. Failaka proved to be full of historical treasures. They included pieces

of red brick found during excavations in Mesopotamia, glazed pottery of Greek origin similar to finds made in Bahrain and the ruins of a Greek temple as Hellenic in detail as the Parthenon built on the hill of the Acropolis at Athens.

The third century BC was suggested by the discovery of a brick-built workshop complete with kiln to make terracotta figures. This was the Seleucid period and the find offered evidence that Failaka was at one time an outpost of the Seleucid empire which, after the death of Alexander the Great, formed almost all of the land mass from the Nile, through Arabia and Persia to India. Stronger evidence of the Seleucid association was later offered by the discovery of the remains of a town, square in outline, on the island. Digs close to the temple produced a hoard of silver coins and one of them bore the likeness of the Syrian King Antiochus, who ruled the Seleucid empire from 223 BC to 187 BC after Alexander. The mail mark of Alexander was found on some of the coins but it was certain they had been minted some hundreds of years after Alexander's death in 323 BC. Historians have established that Alexander's coins were imitated in many outposts of the Greek world long after their minting. Their discovery at Failaka suggests that the island and what is now mainland Kuwait were on the trading route from southern Arabia to the Mediterranean.

Subsequent excavations produced the name Ikaros, engraved on a stone tablet found in the ruins of the temple. Its discovery supported historical evidence that, to the south of the empire of Alexander, there was an outpost,

Above: Archaeological excavations at Failaka Island in Kuwait Bay. There are regular excursions to and from the mainland.
Previous pages: Ground satellite for telecommunications at night. All local telephone calls in Kuwait are free

the small island of Ikaros, near the mouth of the Euphrates, and that island was Failaka. The name of Tylos, another island in the Gulf, has also appeared after extensive researches in the region. This was evidently Bahrain and it is believed that the name "Tylos" could have been derived from Dilmun. In cuneiform script it is easily represented as Dilmun.

About 170 AD, a record of Alexander's campaigns was written and it contained an account of the voyage of a Greek naval leader to a region that is now Pakistan. During his journey he called at two islands, one of them close to the Euphrates, which contained a shrine to Artemis. This was the island Alexander had named Ikaros. Steatite seals found at Failaka produced more evidence to link Ikaros with Tylos (Failaka and Bahrain). One of them was in the still undeciphered Indus script and all were similar to other seals found in Bahrain. Later, intense interest was aroused by new discoveries— pieces of two human figures bearing the cuneiform inscription *Inzak*. A bowl found at Bahrain had been placed in a temple dedicated to Inzak, the god of Dilmun. The temple found at Failaka, however, had been dedicated to Artemis, a gap of 2,000 years from the time of Dilmun.

Thus, it was established that Failaka had been the home of a flourishing community between about 3000 BC to 1200 BC, a period covering the Old Bronze Age (3000 BC to 2100 BC), the Middle Bronze Age (2100 BC to 1600 BC) and the Late Bronze Age (1600 to 1200 BC). The discoveries have been of tremendous importance in trying to trace the history of the earliest civilisations. They included stone seals from the Old Bronze Age, similar in detail to those found in Mesopotamia. The seals produce a clear indication that trade links and political alliances had been established by the people of Failaka and those of the ancient civilisations of the Tigris and Euphrates.

Still, little is known of the history of Failaka and mainland Kuwait between the end of the Bronze Age and the arrival of the forces of Alexander the Great shortly before his death in 323 BC. The Alexandrian troops and their followers established their religion, their architecture and the Greek way of life on the island. Failaka was then Ikaros and Kuwait was called Larissa. The unearthing of the famous stone of Ikaros in the temple ruins proved this when it had been deciphered. The stone contained a message from the second of the Seleucid rulers to the people of Ikaros, clearly named—one of the finest treasures produced by the Greek temple. There were other Greek finds: more stones, statuary and coins. They showed that the people of that time had reached a high level of civilisation. It was evident that Failaka and what is now Kuwait on the mainland were strategic centres at the time of Alexander the Great on the land route to the Arabian hinterland.

It is presumed that the Greek colony finally disappeared following the Roman conquest of the Middle East and the name Ikaros, as time passed, was changed to Failaka. The island was afterwards only sparsely populated and it became a leisure resort for the people of Kuwait. Nevertheless, it remains as a depository of tangible evidence of early history and further excavations may provide important discoveries to bridge the gaps that still exist, particularly to identify the island with Dilmun.

The Dilmun civilisation rose to power about 2800 BC and it dominated the trade routes between Mesopotamia and the ancient cities of the Indus valley until it became part of the Assyrian Empire in 600 BC. Most archaeologists now believe that Bahrain was Dilmun. Discoveries have shown that the first inhabitants date from the Ice Age when northerly regions were still in the process of thawing. Finds of flint implements suggest that the people were Neanderthal but it was with the advent of the Bronze Age (3000 BC) that Bahrain's civilised importance began. It contains the world's largest pre-historic cemetery. An estimated 100,000 burial mounds are located in the north and west of the island and they are believed to date back to the Third Millenium BC. Bahrain has provided three major Bronze Age archaeological sites which contain a temple together with copper and alabaster objects almost identical with similar finds made in the "royal graves" at Ur in Mesopotamia and dating back to 2500 BC.

The Dilmun site is believed to date back 5,000 years. Steatite seals found there are similar to those unearthed at Failaka and elsewhere in the region. They offer solid evidence of trade between the Indus and the Sumerians of Mesopotamia but they were not native to either of these civilisations. It seems certain they were introduced into Mesopotamia and the Indus by traders from what is now Bahrain more than 4,000 years ago. Sumerian literature dated around 2000 BC describes Dilmun as a holy land blessed by Anki, the god of sweet water, and the Sumerian version of The Flood relates how the survivor was granted immortality and settled in Dilmun. Another story, the Epic of Gilgamesh, tells how the survivor went to Dilmun and found immortality there.

Dilmun possessed a highly developed civilisation and its people engaged in extensive trade. Failaka and Kuwait were certainly within the periphery of its far-flung lines of communication.

Sturdy Independence

Kuwait today with its metropolitan sophistication and international prominence is in a totally different dimension—an age away—from the small walled town that had become the symbol of its chequered history and its sturdy independence. The advent of oil riches swept away every vestige of a less well-endowed past. While the architectural evidence of the limited regional role Kuwait used to play has almost entirely been replaced by a vast urbanisation programme, there still remains the spirit of the past—the unquenchable fortitude of the Kuwaiti, his determination to remain free and unfettered, to perpetuate the Islamic heritage of the State and, above all, to give his unstinted loyalty to the Sabah Dynasty whose leadership in the present as in the past guarantees proud nationhood.

From the founding of the original settlement of Kuwait, believed to have taken place about 1710, the name of Sabah has been predominant in historical annals. It is the unifying force, the focal point of loyalty and the protective strength of a fiercely proud and independent people. It has always been so—in more turbulent times in the region, in crisis and in peace. Today, the twelfth Al Sabah Ruler carries on the tradition of enlightened leadership that has always been associated with the family name.

Early in the eighteenth century a group of pure-bred desert dwellers from central Arabia were forced by drought to seek new areas containing pasture and water. After much wandering the group—from the Dahamshah section of the Amarat, a subtribe of the Aniza—reached the southern shore of what is today Kuwait Bay. They found a good supply of sweet water and they stayed. In the group were the ancestors of the Al Sabah, the Ruling Family of Kuwait, and also of the Al Khalifah who are now the Ruling Family of Bahrain. The name of Kuwait was probably derived from the Arabic diminutive of *kut*, a fort, built to protect the early settlers when they decided to establish a permanent home on Kuwait Bay. From that time on the authority of the Al Sabah was supreme and their leadership was never challenged. The first acknowledged Shaikh of the community, Sabah I, assumed leadership in 1756. From that time on the Sabah family have ruled continuously over Kuwait.

In 1764, the Danish explorer, Carsten Niebuhr, visited Kuwait and estimated its population at about 10,000. He told how the inhabitants lived by fishing and pearling, which industry employed more than 800 boats. It was obvious from this account that the settlement had grown in wealth and importance and that, under the Sabah leadership, it had retained its independence in an area dominated by the Ottomans and various powerful Shaikhs.

Kuwaitis travelling in the desert in the early nineteen hundreds

The Ottomans successfully challenged Portuguese supremacy in the Gulf in the sixteenth century and seized Basra and Qatif in 1550. Later, the Portuguese expelled them from Qatif but they remained at Basra and exercised nominal control over most of the land area which is now Iraq. From its earliest years Kuwait had mercantile associations with the Turks in Basra and relations were cordial. The Turks, however, aspired to bring Kuwait under their subjection, an ambition that was never realised though they made several attempts to place the little state under their influence. Finally, Britain's signing of a treaty with Kuwait in 1899 foiled Ottoman hopes of gaining control of Kuwait.

From 1775 to 1779 the Persians, having ousted the Turks from Basra, were in occupation of that important port and trading centre. This diverted much trade to Kuwait and many Basra merchants arrived to carry on business. In addition, the British East India Company sent its mail from India to Kuwait and from there it was carried by camel riders to Aleppo. The camel caravans became known as the "Desert Mail" and covered the journey to Aleppo in from fourteen to twenty days.

In about 1766, during the reign of Abdullah I (1762–1812), the Al-Khalifah family moved southward to Zubara in Qatar. In 1783, the Sabah assisted their kinsmen in driving the Persians from Bahrain and the Al Khalifah became rulers of those islands. Basra was retaken by the Ottomans from the Persians and the turbulence there caused the East India Company to move its factory and staff to Kuwait in 1793. This clearly reflected Kuwaiti independence from Turkish authority. Nevertheless, for Kuwait it was a period of strife. The Wahhabis, a fiercely ascetic religious group enforcing strict and puritanical disciplines, carried out a long series of military conquests from their home in the Nejd and staged several attacks on Kuwait. One assault took place while the East India Company factory was in Kuwait. Cannons were brought ashore from the company's ships and a force of about 500 Wahhabis was repulsed by company troops and the Kuwaitis. As a result the Wahhabis

began to intercept the company's mail couriers and, in 1795, the East India Company officials left Kuwait and the mail again was sent from Zubair, about 150 miles away. Wahhabi pressure continued but Kuwait managed to preserve its precarious independence and to remain free from Ottoman interference.

By 1830, the town extended for about a mile along the shore of Kuwait Bay. Shaikh Jabir I (1812–1859) had succeeded his father, Abdullah, and he maintained friendly relations with Britain which then, anxious to preserve valuable trading routes with India, was playing an important role in the Gulf region. In 1859, Shaikh Sabah II, who died in 1866, became the Ruler of Kuwait which had, by that time, a population of about 20,000. It had established its reputation as a busy trading centre and seaport and the fame of its seafaring community spread far and wide. Kuwait had become the most important port in the northern part of the Gulf and its ships ventured far to increase the prosperity of the town where the desert met the sea and where the desert dweller, the merchant and the seaman worked in harmonious industry under the stable Sabah administration.

The Ruling Family, mindful of its own desert background, maintained traditional links with the Bedouin, upholding the desert code of honour and chivalry. Thus they obtained the loyalty of the free-moving tribes and, at the same time, maintained a sophisticated urban leadership which welded both desert-dweller and townsman in amicable association.

Shaikh Sabah II was followed by Shaikh Abdullah II (1866–1892) and then by a period when the Ottomans, occupying what is now Iraq, aspired to increase their power in Kuwait. On Abdullah's death Shaikh Muhammad

A traditional desert scene: camels heading for camp

(1892–1896) ascended to power. For Kuwait this meant troubled times. Muhammad showed no sign of the Sabah strength and political wisdom, and Turkish interference in Kuwaiti affairs clearly showed that a takeover was planned. Raiding and plundering increased outside Kuwait town and Kuwait was rapidly plunging into a state of lawlessness.

It was in this time of crisis that a man of strength and vision appeared in the person of Mubarak, half-brother of Muhammad. He hated Muhammad's pro-Turkish policy, which threatened the independence of Kuwait, and he spoke out fearlessly against the incompetent leadership. As a result, he was banished into the desert with instructions to restore order there if he could —a mission that was likely to lead to his death. In the desert, Mubarak was without money or supplies but he rallied to his cause some of the boldest tribal leaders and carried out a successful campaign against rebellious elements. He appealed to Muhammad for money and support to continue his mission of restoring order but was refused.

There was only one course left open: to seize power and reassert Kuwait's independent existence. In a bold and carefully planned raid Mubarak and his small band of followers killed Muhammad and his brother, Jarrah. Muhammad's pro-Turkish Wazir fled to Ottoman territory and Mubarak prepared himself to meet the people seated on the throne of the large majlis council room of the shaikhs on the site now occupied by the new Seif Palace, the administrative headquarters of the Amir. Though stunned at the news of the death of Muhammad and Jarrah, the elders, who had expected to pay their respects to Muhammad, accepted the *fait accompli;* the news brought

15

16

crowds to the majlis where they acclaimed Mubarak as their new ruler.

Mubarak wasted no time in asserting the independence of Kuwait and this brought heavy Turkish pressure on him and his people. The Turks bestowed on Mubarak a title. He spurned it. He imposed a levy on imports, including those of Turkish origin. When the Ottomans sent an official and soldiers to take charge of Kuwait port he made approaches to Britain but found that the British government was not ready to offend Turkey. In 1899, however, fearing German expansion in the area through a treaty with Turkey and apprehensive of Imperial Russian designs in the Gulf, Britain signed a treaty with Kuwait guaranteeing predominant British interest in the State. This aroused Turkish resentment and, three years later, a warship was sent to Kuwait with an ultimatum that Mubarak should allow Turkish troops to be stationed in the port or abdicate. Mubarak refused. Britain sent three naval vessels to Kuwait and landed a small force of soldiers. After a Turkish-inspired attempt to kill Mubarak was foiled by townspeople under arms and by a British warship no further attempts were made to overthrow Shaikh Mubarak.

In June 1904, the first British Political Agent was appointed to Kuwait and this marked the consolidation of Kuwaiti-British friendship. Britain assured Shaikh Mubarak that it recognised Kuwait's independence and the ruler's right and desire to keep sole control of the internal administration of the State. Mubarak proved to be a wise and stable ruler and it was as Shaikh Mubarak the Great that he was remembered after his death. The title was well earned for he was strong, upright and decisive. Until his death in 1915 Kuwait maintained its stalwart independence—a legacy that was firmly upheld by the Sabah line which followed him.

In 1891, the Al Saud who had established themselves in the Nejd were forced to flee after Turkish intervention placed their hereditary enemies, the Ibn Rashid of Hail, in command of Riyahd. Shaikh Mubarak granted the Amir Abdul-Rahman Ibn Faisal Al Saud permission to live in exile in Kuwait with his four sons the eldest of whom, Abdul-Aziz, was later to become King Ibn Saud. In 1902, Abdul Aziz, no doubt inspired by the daring exploit which had placed Mubarak in power in Kuwait, led a small band of followers to Riyadh where the Rashidi governor was killed and he took possession of the city. Later, Shaikh Mubarak continued to give full support to Abdul-Aziz Ibn Saud who extended his power over the whole of the Nejd. Finally, all the hereditary Saud domains were recaptured.

Under Mubarak's rule Kuwait's seafaring and mercantile trade expanded.

Above left: A street scene in the old Kuwait. Below left and right: The dhow, now equipped with outboard motor, still plies the trade route to India and beyond. At one time the entire commercial life of Kuwait depended upon these boats

The town became the centre of a prosperous community and the home of many skilled craftsmen whose fame spread throughout the region. Law and order were strictly maintained and the reputation of Kuwait's citizens for absolute honesty was recorded in the chronicles of several European travellers exploring the Gulf region. In 1914, the State's population was about 35,000 concentrated mostly in the town which contained more than 3,000 houses and about 500 shops. Prosperity came from Kuwait's position as a trading centre, from shipping and shipbuilding, fishing and pearling and, on a smaller scale, camel breeding. More than 500 boats with crews of from 15 to 50 men were engaged in pearl fishing and much larger vessels carried on a profitable trade with India and Africa.

After the death of Shaikh Mubarak the rise in central Arabia of a dynamic force known as the Ikhwan (Brethren) produced turbulent times in the region and the tenacity of Kuwaiti citizens was often put to the test. The Ikhwan, who had revived the religious zeal of the Wahhabis, believed themselves to be God's instrument for restoring the purity of the Islamic faith. With militant fervour they set out to attack the domains of the peoples they classed as "infidels".

Jabir II (1915–1917), the eldest son of Mubarak, followed his father as Shaikh. Jabir in turn was followed by Salim (1917–1921). Relations with Ibn Saud had deteriorated as a result of inter-tribal disputes over suzerainty rights. The Nejd ruler had become the leader of the Ikhwan and, in 1917, he undertook punitive action against tribes which would not accept Ikhwanism. A powerful Ikhwan army under its chief, Faisal al Duwish, had been formed and had given its support to Ibn Saud who was then engaged in a long and bitter dispute over border territories with Shaikh Salim. The confrontation erupted into hostilities when the Ikhwan fell upon a Kuwaiti force and almost wiped it out. Shaikh Salim immediately ordered the construction of a defensive wall around Kuwait town and this was completed in the remarkable time of two months. The achievement was a forerunner of Kuwait's staggeringly rapid transformation after the advent of oil.

Late in 1920, a large Ikhwan force attacked Jahra, the site of a small oasis outside the town. Considerably outnumbered, the Kuwaitis were forced to withdraw to the Red Fort—The Qasr Al Ahmar—now preserved as one of the State's links with the past. The Ikhwan launched attack after attack against the fort but were held off by the waterless garrison and finally, after suffering grievous losses, had to withdraw. The Battle of Jahra is commemorated

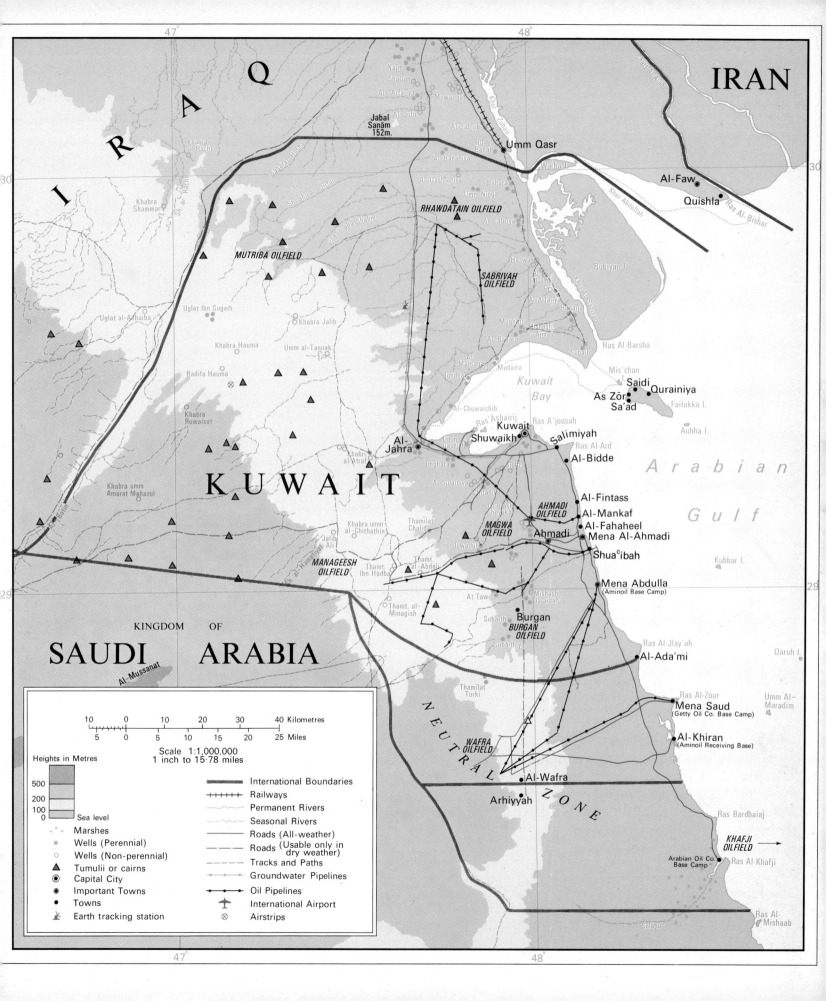

IRAQ

IRAN

KUWAIT

KINGDOM OF
SAUDI ARABIA

Arabian
Gulf

NEUTRAL ZONE

Jabal
Sanām
152m.

Umm Qasr

Al-Faw
Quishla

RHAWDATAIN OILFIELD

MUTRIBA OILFIELD

SABRIYAH
OILFIELD

Kuwait
Bay

Saidi
As Zōr   Qurainiya
Sa'ad

Al-Jahra

Kuwait
Shuwaikh   Salimiyah
Al-Bidde

Al-Fintass
AHMADI
OILFIELD   Al-Mankaf
MAGWA   Al-Fahaheel
OILFIELD   Mena Al-Ahmadi
Ahmadi
Shua°ibah

MANAGEESH
OILFIELD   Mena Abdulla
(Aminoil Base Camp)

Burgan
BURGAN
OILFIELD
Al-Ada'mi

Ras Al-Zour
Mena Saud
(Getty Oil Co. Base Camp)

WAFRA
OILFIELD   Al-Khiran
(Aminoil Receiving Base)

Al-Wafra
Arhiyyah

Ras Bardhaiaj

KHAFJI
OILFIELD

Arabian Oil Co.
Base Camp   Ras Al-Khafji

Ras Al-
Mishaab

10   0   10   20   30   40 Kilometres

5   0   5   10   15   20   25 Miles

Scale 1:1,000,000
1 inch to 15·78 miles

Heights in Metres

500
200
100
0   Sea level

Marshes
Wells (Perennial)
Wells (Non-perennial)
Tumulii or cairns
Capital City
Important Towns
Towns
Earth tracking station
Airstrips

International Boundaries
Railways
Permanent Rivers
Seasonal Rivers
Roads (All-weather)
Roads (Usable only in
        dry weather)
Tracks and Paths
Groundwater Pipelines
Oil Pipelines
International Airport

today and the old fort stands amid the huge office blocks as a monument to Kuwaiti steadfastness and courage.

Shaikh Salim was succeeded by his nephew, Shaikh Ahmad (1921–1950). Ibn Saud immediately declared that he had no further quarrel with Kuwait but the frontier problem remained unsolved and, under the aegis of Britain, at a crucial desert meeting at Uqair, the territories of Iraq, Kuwait and what is now Saudi Arabia were delineated. At the southern and western extremities of Kuwait two neutral zones were marked on the map. These areas provided buffer territory for all the states, giving equal access to fresh water and grazing land. Despite the loss of some territory, Kuwait maintained close relations with Britain, although the frontier conference had left much bitterness in the State. Shaikh Ahmad set up a council of advisers drawn from prominent merchants in the town but, in all matters, his word was law.

At the Uqair conference in 1922, Kuwait was represented by Major J. C. More, the British Political Agent in Kuwait, while both Iraq and Saudi Arabia sent their own representatives to the conference which was dominated by Sir Percy Cox, the High Commissioner in Baghdad. After much hard bargaining the new borders of Kuwait were defined by a line which started at the junction of Wadi al 'Aujah and the Batin valley in the west to the point where the 29th parallel of latitude met the border of Najd (Saudi Arabia) and Kuwait. It then followed the same line to a coastal point just south of Ras al Qalai'ah (Jlay'ah). South of this boundary was the Kuwait Neutral Zone. It meant that Kuwait had been deprived of nearly two-thirds of its territory. Shaikh Admad was dismayed and his faith in Britain was shaken; he called it the sacrifice of a small nation to a greater power.

There followed a period of privation for Kuwait when the Saudis imposed a blockade against the State and by 1930 there was a severe economic depression. It was a time of hostilities involving Ibn Saud and the Ikhwan who

Above and below left: The traditional skills of dhow construction have not been lost. Below: The shoreline of the old Kuwait in the early nineteen hundreds

Above: The nomadic way of life was sustained for centuries, as people crossed the desert with camels and goats. Above and below right: Traditional scenes of the old Kuwait, taken in the early nineteen hundreds

rose in rebellion against his authority. They came close to overthrowing Saudi power but were finally subdued when Kuwait refused them refuge in its territory. The Saudi blockade continued for seven years, from 1922 to 1929. But when it ended Kuwait's troubles were not over and there was a long succession of land-ownership disputes with Iraqi interests. Much later, in 1961, Kuwait had again to face Iraqi claims for Kuwait territory on the grounds that the State had been part of Basra province under Ottoman rule. With the support of Britain these claims were rejected by Kuwait.

With the establishment of peace in the region there came the rush of oil prospectors and in Kuwait in 1934 the Kuwait Oil Company was formed as an Anglo-American enterprise with British Petroleum (then the Anglo-Persian Oil Company) and the Gulf Oil Corporation of America as partners operating on a concession granted by Shaikh Ahmad to search for and produce oil in the State. Promising drilling results were obtained but the outbreak of World War II caused a suspension of operations. Kuwait gave active support to the Allies during the war but was not involved in hostilities.

After the war, the Kuwait Oil Company established its headquarters at Ahmadi close to Burgan where a large oil reservoir had been found. The name of the town commemorates Shaikh Ahmad's role in establishing the industry which was to transform the State's economy from the basis of pearling and dhow trading to one built on its vast underground treasure-house of oil. Shaikh Ahmad died on January 29, 1950—the first Ruler of Kuwait's oil era. He was the last of the traditionalist Shaikhs and though he regretted that the old tribal customs and desert kinship would, inevitably, be influenced by the advent of untold wealth and the social changes that affluence would introduce, he accepted the need for the development of the industry in the belief, rightly so, that it would benefit every inhabitant of the country.

The transformation of Kuwait had begun under his rule. New schools had been built and a government hospital was constructed to supplement the facilities of the first hospital in Kuwait run by American missionaries. Gradually, the character of Kuwait was changing—from a dhow port and trading centre to a thriving modern metropolis supported by the revenues of the oil industry. By 1950, the population had risen to about 150,000. The new Ruler, Shaikh Abdullah III (1950–1965) was a cousin of Shaikh Ahmad and the son of a former Ruler, Shaikh Salim. He carried on the benevolent administration of Shaikh Ahmad and it was under his guidance that Kuwait

24

The old Political Agency in Kuwait City, June 1904

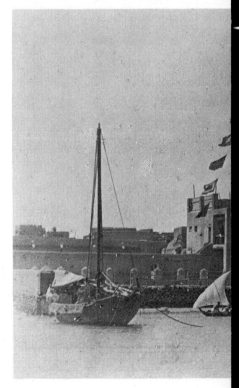

became a fully sovereign state under the terms of the 1961 treaty with Britain. Thus the last of the line of British Political Agents, Sir John Richmond, became Britain's first Ambassador accredited to Shaikh Abdullah who assumed the title of Amir.

The national flag, made up of green, white and red stripes in association with a black trapezoid, replaced the earlier inscribed white-on-red ensign. A provisional government was established with an appointed constituent assembly and a draft constitution was drawn up for the State. This was approved by the Amir in 1962 and the first general election for a National Assembly was held the following year. The country was divided into ten regions and each member of the electorate had five votes. The Assembly was elected with the power to veto government policies on a free vote. Alone the Amir enjoyed constitutional immunity. It was a great leap forward bridging the gulf between hereditary tribal rule and universal suffrage and it reflected the immense change in the country's economic fortunes.

In 1958, the Hashemite regime in Iraq was overthrown and General Qassem came to power. In 1961 he declared that Kuwait was "an inseparable part of Iraq" and tension increased steadily in the border area. Kuwait was given the support of the Arab League and Saudi Arabia offered its fraternal assistance. Britain had made it clear that Kuwait would be protected. Warships were sent to the State and a British military force was landed. Gradually, the threat was lifted though the Iraq claim was reiterated by General Qassem.

When Shaikh Abdullah died Kuwait had emerged as a modern state worthy of its growing international importance. Its schools and hospitals had become the pride of the Arab world, a constitutional democracy had been established, a strong independent currency was in use and diplomatic relations had been established with most foreign countries. Kuwait was a member of the Arab League and its full international status as a sovereign power was recognised by its admission to the United Nations in 1963.

Kuwait's present Amir, Sabah III, has continued the family tradition of wise statesmanship and administrative wisdom and the importance of the country in international affairs today, its enlightened democracy, its massive social-welfare pattern and its generous aid to poorer nations are all hallmarks of the Sabah heritage which, in unbroken line, has been the paternal focal point of unswerving loyalty throughout the State's chequered history.

Liberal Democracy

Right: A dramatic aerial view of Kuwait City

Kuwait's Constitution is a remarkably liberal document on which has been founded a truly democratic State. It lays down such obvious principles as the sovereignty and Arabic character of the State, the pre-eminence of Islam and Islamic law, the priority of Arabic as the official language and the obligatory use of flag, emblems and other symbols of nationhood but it also ensures complete religious freedom for all sections of the population and personal liberty is fully guaranteed.

The Constitution guarantees the freedom of the Press. The care and protection of the young are the subject of specific requirements, and discrimination on the grounds of race, social origin, language or religion invites severe penalties. There is freedom to join trade unions or to contract out of them. The Amir is named as the constitutional ruler and as Commander-in-Chief of the armed forces. He may declare war by decree but the Constitution specifically forbids participation in an offensive war and only permits the mobilisation of the armed forces for defence of the realm. All the freedoms enshrined in the Constitution are watched over by an independent judiciary.

The Prime Minister is appointed by the Amir and there is a nominated Council of Ministers who are answerable to the elected National Assembly, where a vote of no confidence can force their resignations. The Council of Ministers can thus be compelled to submit its policies to the scrutiny of the Assembly. The National Assembly is formed of members elected in a general election held every four years and there is an elected President who performs the role of Speaker in the British Parliament. The Assembly is composed of 50 elected members—Deputies—to whom the Ministers are answerable for all policies. Administratively, the State is divided into three Governorates: the Capital Governorate, the Hawalli Governorate and the Ahmadi Governorate.

Following the general election held in January 1975, the list of ministries was:

Education

Housing

Liberal Democracy   Public Works
Social Affairs and Labour
Interior and Defence
Transport
Foreign Affairs
Finance
Public Health
Justice, Awqaf (Religious Endowments) and Islamic Affairs
Electricity and Water
Oil
Commerce and Industry
Ministry of State for Cabinet Affairs

The Prime Minister and the Deputy Prime Minister, who is also Minister of Information, complete the list. Three new ministries were created after the election: Oil (which was formerly associated with the Ministry of Finance and Oil), Transport and Housing.

All Kuwaiti males over the age of twenty-one have the right to vote. There are no political parties but the history of Parliamentary government and the size of the country make it easy for democracy to be practised. Public opinion is reflected in the National Assembly and in the Press.

Right: The commercial
area in downtown Kuwait

Above: Shaikh Jabir Al Ahmed Al Jabir as-Sabah, the Heir Apparent and Prime Minister of Kuwait. Left: A morning audience (the Majlis) with the Head of State of Kuwait at his administrative head-quarters, the Seif Palace. All Kuwaitis have the right to approach their ruler. Right: The National Assembly in Ordinary Session

Merchants, Mariners, Craftsmen

Old Kuwait and new Kuwait appear to be an age apart but there is no need to delve into ancient historical chronicles to discover where the difference lies. No more than twenty-five years ago old Kuwait existed, the small walled town and seaport that was the symbol of a less affluent age. The staggering transformation from the past to the metropolitan present, from mudbrick to concrete and steel, from narrow lanes to multi-laned speedways, occurred well within living memory. In comparison with the evolutionary progress of much older countries, Kuwait's metamorphosis has been phenomenal, not only architecturally but in bestowing the gift of new-found riches to create a new social order which is the envy of many today.

Yet old Kuwait was, on a smaller scale, a regionally prosperous state founded on the industriousness of its population who had earned an enviable reputation as skilled craftsmen, seafarers, pearl-divers and merchants. Few traces of that time now exist in modern Kuwait but in the minds of many the memories of the pre-oil era are still vivid. The old scene can still be recalled by young men who were children when the first rush of oil signalled what must be one of the most rapid transformations of an entire country ever seen anywhere in the world.

Kuwait in the 1930s had a population of about 60,000 and the town extended about four miles along the shore of the bay and about two miles inland at its densest central part. The fortified wall enclosed the town on the southern side and there was a wide, open space between the limits of the built-up area and the wall at the east end. There were situated small market gardens growing vegetables. Nearby clay had been dug for building or gypsum had been uncovered. There were two Arab cemeteries and a small Christian cemetery. It was a town of narrow, meandering streets and there was no alignment of the houses. Pathways between the houses had been trodden by the donkeys, horses, and camels which carried such necessities as water contained in goatskins, dried palm fronds for firewood, charcoal or kerosene. The common building material was mud, either applied wet to build up a wall or as sun-dried bricks, and the general colour of the town was a dark, sandy yellow unrelieved by any touch of greenery or vegetation. Houses, usually

Left: Pearl fishing was the principle industry of Kuwait before the oil boom

33

Merchants, Mariners, Craftsmen

A sea-going boum coming in to shore

built round courtyards, were mostly one storey high but, here and there, upper rooms would stand in prominence above the general level of the house-tops.

In the well-to-do households—and there were many in the prosperous port and trading centre—life proceeded in quarters round the courtyards. There the housewife, her children, unmarried female relatives and serving girls would go about their daily tasks. In some of the houses there was a second courtyard where the head of the family could entertain his friends away from the female quarters. At the entrance to the male domain there was always a coffee room and benches were often set outside the main door so that the men could sit and chat and catch the evening breeze. The Naif and Jahra gates in the fortified wall provided access at the western end for traffic to and from the desert. On that side of the town there was a large encampment of black tents pitched there by the desert-dwellers, some inside, some outside the wall.

The famous Nayef Palace with its 15-foot walls stood sentinel immediately inside the wall. This was then the headquarters of the Shaikh's men-at-arms and contained their arsenal of weapons, mostly rifles. In its vast courtyard today stand the gallows where criminals convicted and sentenced to death for murder are hanged. Usually, clemency is bestowed and the death sentence is commuted but, in the case of particularly brutal killings, the supreme penalty is imposed. Entering the town by the Naif gate and past the fort, one found the busy market square where the man from the desert conducted his business with the townspeople. Camels and sheep were offered for sale and caravans were loaded with goods for the interior. North of the square the shops catered for Bedouin needs. Women, clad in traditional black and veiled, mingled with the predominantly male crowds in the streets, usually on their way to the women's market which specialised in cloth-lengths and items of jewellery.

The main business district was situated in the market area where a long, covered street lined with shops ran to the Customs wharf on the seafront. In the honeycomb of alleyways running off the main street were the workshops of the skilled craftsmen, the shops of the carpet-sellers, the gold-dealers, the pearl merchants and many others. Near the seafront the wholesale dealers in rice, coffee, tea, sugar and other commodities had built warehouses. The seafront scene provided a picturesque contrast with the town. The entire shoreline contained boats of every description, some of them in various stages of construction. By the waterside stood steel capstans and wooden water-tanks. White sails were spread on the ground for sailmakers to sew. On every side were the industry and craftsmanship that had made Kuwait the finest boat-building centre in the Gulf.

The seafront also contained a series of small harbours and there was a continual traffic of boats coming and going—small dhows engaged in local commerce, medium-sized boums bringing Kuwait's precious supplies of fresh water from the Shatt Al Arab, the lighters taking cargoes ashore from the big steamers and the fishing fleet. The ocean-going boums, some as big as 300 tons, were the pride of the Kuwaiti shipbuilders. They made the annual trading voyages, which lasted from six to eight months in the winter season of the north-east monsoon in the Indian Ocean. They collected cargoes of dates from Iraq and followed one of two traditional courses either down the Gulf along the coast of Baluchistan to Karachi and then southward to Cochin or Calicut where they loaded timber for the return, or down the Arabian coast calling at ports down to Aden and from there to East Africa as far as Zanzibar. Principal return cargoes were mangrove poles used for roofing houses in Kuwait.

Up to the 1930s pearling was Kuwait's major industry with up to about 800 boats engaged in the regular exodus to the pearling grounds in the Gulf. Up to 15,000 men were employed in the industry and in the 1920s it was worth around $1 million in revenue annually. Every summer the pearling fleet set off for the southern pearling grounds. The proceeds of pearling were divided among the crews of the boats, the captains and divers receiving three shares and the sailors two shares. For the merchants there was profit but for the divers it was a hazardous and gruelling occupation requiring long periods of immersion in the water, where there were intense pressures. In many instances the diver's life was a short one.

The diver usually wore only a loin cloth and a leather protector over his fingers. He descended rapidly on a heavy stone to the sea-bed, his nostrils closed with a wooden clip. He carried a knife to cut the oyster from the bottom and worked at high speed while his breath lasted, placing the oysters in a small basket attached to his neck. He surfaced unaided and, after a short rest, would go down again with the stone which the crew would then haul to the surface once he had reached the sea-bed. All the oysters were placed in a heap on the deck of each ship and in the evening or on the following morning they were opened by all hands to see what they contained. Strict rituals were observed. Haulers and divers remained separated and an oyster was never opened until the appointed time. A copy of the Holy Koran wrapped in cloth was always hung at the stern of each boat and was taken down in the evenings for the captain to read passages to his crew.

In the heyday of the industry practically every family in Kuwait had a stake. Its importance was reflected in the presence of the Shaikh at the pearl banks at the end of the season when he gave the signal for the fleet to return home. Sails were hoisted and course set for Kuwait where the wives and

families of the men, who had been away for four months, gathered at the seafront in their best clothes to welcome the boats home with drums and waving banners. The decline of pearling had a damaging effect on Kuwait's economy but one which lasted only a relatively short time. The discovery of oil in abundance was not far away and, as an industry, it eclipsed in magnitude anything that had been seen before. It marked the end of an era of meagre resources and the disappearance of the small, walled town that had left its indelible mark on the history of the region.

Merchants, Mariners, Craftsmen

The Great Leap

The advent of oil has produced a new Kuwait—a vast latter-day sprawl of office blocks, residential areas, industrial sites and recreational spaces that have advanced far beyond the old town wall—demolished in 1957—to provide a much larger population with such amenities as supermarkets and stores, cinemas and sports stadiums, on what within living memory was a vast expanse of open desert. All this has been accomplished with astonishing speed and efficiency in no more than twenty-five years. Only a few buildings of architectural and historical interest now remain of the old days. Kuwait

Below: A general view of
Kuwait City

Left: A street scene showing the traditional architecture of the old Kuwait. Below: A large house in a residential area of the city. These modern houses are well serviced by nearby shopping centres

has swept away the memory of the limited resources and smallness of the past and in its place has built one of the most modern urban centres in the world.

Oil brought a vast influx of foreigners—mostly Arab. Kuwait's population today is cosmopolitan but it remains largely Arab and Islamic in character with more than 300 mosques perpetuating the classical Arabian pattern of architecture in the midst of the vast spread of concrete and steel on the western style. Thus the various sections of the population are linked by a common Arabic background and Islam. Yet ancestral customs remain distinctive and social traits varied. The last census—in April 1970—revealed that there were more than 391,000 non-Kuwaitis living in the State. In 1957, the total was just over 73,500. Eight years later it has risen to more than 247,000. In 1970 the total population, including Kuwaitis, was 738,662—with Kuwaitis making up 47 per cent. Of the non-Kuwaitis, the Palestinians (many of them from Jordan) formed the largest group at more than 147,000. Other Arab groups came from all over the Arab world.

Estimates of the population at the end of 1973 placed the total at more than 907,000 with 407,000 Kuwaitis living alongside a non-Kuwaiti section of nearly 500,000. At the end of 1975 the projection was that total population

Below: Goat herding outside the city gates in olden days. Right: The Shamiyah Gate, a vestige of the city's ramparts through which we can see the modern telecommunications tower—home of the telephone service

Above and right: The
Seif Palace, the Amir's
administrative headquarters

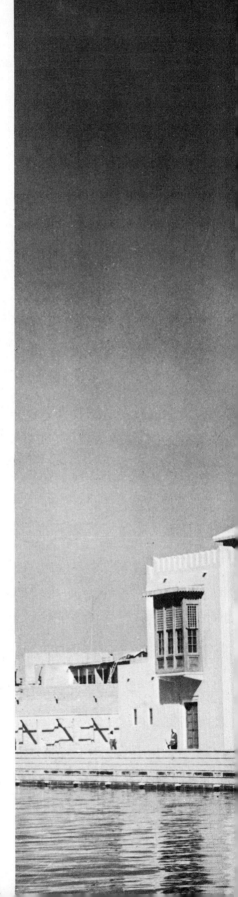

would reach about 972,500, comprising more than 532,000 non-Kuwaitis and about 440,000 Kuwaitis. By the year 2000 the forecast envisaged a population of more than three million with non-Kuwaitis still in the majority. Variants of this total exist but they all place the total population at well over two million.

The Kuwaitis themselves remain distinctively traditional in retaining their patriotic identity with the past. Fostered by the example of the ruling family they maintain the Kuwaiti dress of bisht (cloak) over dishdasha (gown) with the ghatra (headdress) held secure by the ugal (black cord). The majority of the remainder of the population wear western-style clothes but Arabic is the *lingua franca* with English in second place. Automobiles and wide multi-laned highways have replaced the narrow streets of the past. Modern technology has brought electricity and water in abundance where once there was scarcity. Air-conditioning, television and radio, computers—all the products of a scientific age—may be found where once donkeys, horses and camels provided the only means of transportation. The change has truly

Above: An old picture of the Souk (market).
Above right: Friends camping in the desert during the spring school holidays partake of lemon flavoured tea or strong bitter coffee from small cups. Below right: A Kuwaiti family takes coffee and tea at home. Below extreme right: A residential suburb of Kuwait City. Overleaf above left and right: Fahed Al-Salem street, the heart of the business district. Overleaf below left: An aerial view of Kuwait City.

48

been phenomenal and reflects the wisdom of the ruling family and government in bestowing the benefits of oil riches on the entire population.

Kuwait remains a predominantly masculine society but the advance of women to educational and social equality has been rapidly accomplished. There is still the contrast between old and new, between tradition and liberalism, in the scene set by the intermingling of the conservative, black-garbed women with their veils and those who have followed modern fashion trends on the western pattern. Educationally, Kuwait's women have leapt forward. Girl students are in the majority at the University and, in comparison with the 140 girls attending school in 1937 there were nearly 60,000 in government schools in 1973–74. Women are also prominent in Kuwait's commercial life and in the government service. Up to the present only Kuwaiti males over the age of twenty-one have the right to vote but several women's organisations, with male backing, are proposing women's suffrage and the expansion of opportunities for females.

This is a reflection of the duality of Kuwait society. Traditionalism remains strong, mostly in the older generation, but there is a strong and growing liberal element, formed mostly by those who have come into contact with western ideas. Basically the groups represent the old desert tribal culture and the modern, urban population. There is, however, no conflict beyond the debating level and both sections are loyal to the Sabah rulers who are, as in the past, the unifying force. The contrast between past and present is vividly presented by the traffic scene in Kuwait City which, as in other metropolitan areas of the world, has brought the rush-hour crawl, the inevitable traffic jams and the perennial problem of parking to a place where the automobile was not so long ago a rarity indeed.

In April 1974, according to the General Director of Traffic, Kuwait Police, there were 215,566 motor vehicles using the country's 1,000 miles of main roads. Every year the police must anticipate an increase of 40,000 automobiles of every description adding to the problem of congestion. Yet, in 1960 there were only 33,201 vehicles on the roads. Last year there were 235,212 licensed drivers. All this creates one of the thickest densities of traffic seen anywhere in the world, comparable with the present-day scene in such cities as Tokyo, London or New York. In order to cope with the increasing problem of traffic density Kuwait has undertaken a vast programme of new road building in the urban area. This includes a four-lane highway built on reclaimed land which traverses the whole length of the shore-line for about

fifteen kilometres. It will syphon off commuter traffic between the residential areas and the business centre from vastly overloaded highways.

Roundabouts, which handled the traffic flow efficiently for several years, have now been outdated by the heavy flow of vehicles. In their place have come traffic lights. Some of these were well on the way to completion at the end of 1974. The Police Traffic Department is being rapidly expanded and new premises equipped with the latest technical equipment are being provided. Parking has been tackled as a problem of extreme urgency and with a probable half-million vehicles on the roads in the near future multi-storey car parks are under construction. In addition, open spaces, formerly the sites of old houses, have been reserved for car-owners in the city centre.

Above and right: Fahed Al-Salem Mosque in Salmiyah differs from the more traditional Mosques by its modern design. Devout Kuwaitis visit the Mosques five times a day

54

In contrast with the recent past Kuwait will shortly have a modern school for the training of traffic policemen. It will be equipped with simulators and the latest technical aids. This will be part of the new headquarters of the branch and other buildings will be constructed in other parts of the State. There will be a testing station for vehicles and a factory for the production of standardised number plates. So far as manpower is concerned the Traffic Section has recruited men with special skills—traffic engineers, civil engineers, electronics experts and business administrators as well as the uniformed men who will also be highly trained. This, it is hoped, will reduce the accident rate which is high. In Kuwait the average is about 12,000 every year with 300 fatal injuries and 3,000 casualties.

In built-up areas there is a 45 kph speed limit and 70–80 maximum on the main highways. The total of public buses at the end of 1973 was 1,644. This service is still being expanded by the addition of several hundred new vehicles. There were also 1,170 private buses and 15,776 private trucks. Nearly 7,000 taxis were operating in various areas of the State, mostly in the Kuwait City district. Kuwait does not possess a railway or tramway system, but as a means to provide rapid transit to and from the built-up areas the planners have proposed the construction of a railway link between Kuwait City and Fahaheel, 35 kilometres away, with some of the track going underground. A monorail has also been suggested.

Since the days of the dhows Kuwait port has been transformed into a modern complex of docks and warehouses with the latest equipment for speedy handling of cargoes. In 1973, the tonnage discharged at Shuwaikh port totalled nearly 1,400,000 tons with 1,161 ships of a total tonnage of more than 4.5 million tons using the port. Of these 87 were of Kuwaiti registry. The United Kingdom (152) and Japan (124) were the biggest users of the port facilities. Similarly, Kuwait's International Airport has seen a rapid increase in aircraft arrivals since 1965 when the total was 6,642. In 1973, this had increased to 7,387. Departures were on a similar scale. The airport, which is due for enlargement in view of increasing traffic, handles a wide variety of international flights and the jets of the world's leading airlines maintain regular services to Europe, the United States, the Far East and the Middle East region. The airport is connected to Kuwait City by a wide, brilliantly lit motorway which is, day and night, one of the busiest arteries of new Kuwait.

The state's economic position in the world has meant a constant stream

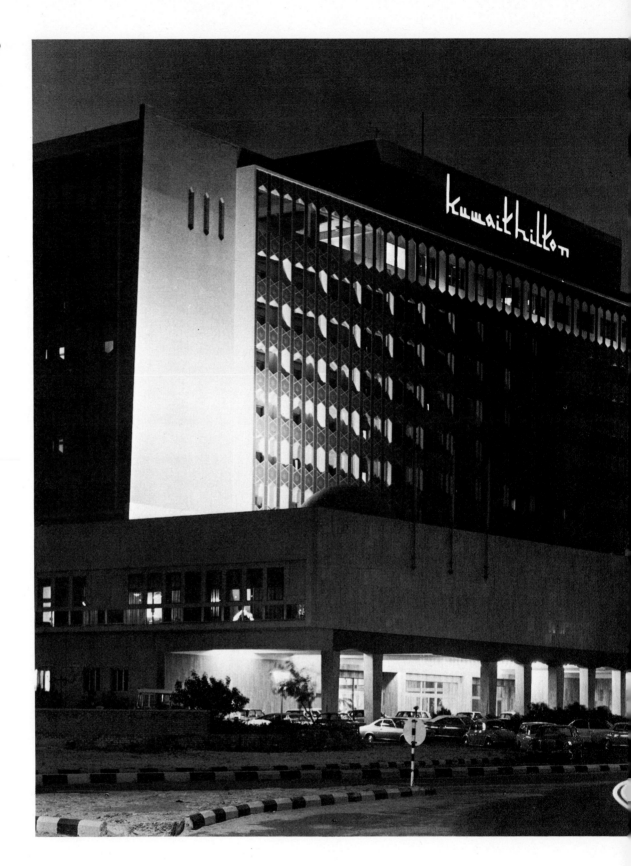

The Kuwait Hilton, built
in 1968 on the seafront

of visitors and hotel accommodation is often at a premium though more than 1,000 rooms are available in seventeen hotels. There are two luxury-class and six first-class establishments, the remainder operating on a smaller scale. By 1973, after ten years of demolition and new building, Kuwait had about 10,000 houses, including luxury residences and groups of low-income villas built by the government and offered at exceptionally low rentals. Generous compensation was paid to those whose old houses were demolished to make way for the new city and a state mortgage scheme enabled Kuwaitis to buy homes without deposit at 2 per cent interest over 25 years. Building contractors received finance from the government and, as a result, the transformation of the city was pushed ahead at an amazingly rapid rate.

Some idea of the almost overnight change may be gauged from statistics: a total of 8,308 low income houses were built between 1964 and 1967 with large blocks of flats and luxury residences mushrooming along the seafront. By the mid-sixties there were 7 cinemas (there are now 10 with more being built), 41 kindergartens, 76 primary, 51 intermediate, 10 secondary and 17 other schools, 10 hospitals, 38 medical clinics, 38 dental centres, 11 child and mother welfare centres, 195 school health clinics, 249 industrial establishments and 32 hotels and lodging houses. Between 1966 and 1968, 17,000 construction permits were issued—everywhere building changed the landscape from the past to the bustling present. The expansion, the building, the changing of the face of Kuwait still proceeds. By the end of 1973, 6,007 low-income houses had been built and distributed in Kuwait City. There were another 5,050 in the Hawalli Governorate and others elsewhere made a grand total of 13,569. Planned for the future—many of them built now—were 18,872 more, a prime example of the social welfare benefits enjoyed by the population. Nowhere in these vast low-income estates can rent exceed 5 per cent of the tenants' total income.

The keystone in this expansion has been the government's urban development programme and land-purchase scheme. Kuwaitis were evacuated from the old walled town while vast new suburbs, extending in regular blocks of up to 10 kilometres, were built in what was then bare desert. Between January 1952 and April 1971, a total of Kuwaiti Dinars 697.5 million (more than US $2 billion) had been disbursed to Kuwaitis through the property acquisition scheme principally in the old town. The majority were allocated plots of land 750 or 1,000 metres square on a lottery system organised by the municipality. With the money paid as compensation for the loss of their old

The Great Leap   houses or with cheap government loans, the Kuwaitis were then enabled to build homes to their own tastes in "super blocks" equipped with centrally placed shopping areas, schools, mosques, meeting halls and social clubs.

Certainly today Shaikh Ahmad would not recognise the Kuwait that his signing of the oil concession created. The speed was breathtaking. The past disappeared in a massive explosion of constructional activity. A modern metropolis appeared with all the amenities for a pampered population— plentiful water supplies, air-conditioning and central heating, regular power supplies, supermarkets, cinemas, social clubs, sports stadiums, colour television, world-wide telecommunications . . . all the gadgetry of the space age. Yet only 25 years previously there was old Kuwait, small, meagre of resources, a place of traditional shortages and small, traditional crafts. Yet some legacies of the past remain as architectural monuments of Kuwait's Arab identity.

The wall was one of the first structures to go but the gates that allowed passage through the wall remain as monuments now engulfed by the massive structures which have spread far beyond the old boundaries. The old Political Agency building on the seafront still stands. The palatial house built by Shaikh Khazal of Muhammerah in 1890 remains, with what was once the harem now occupied by a merchant family and the other portion as a museum. The Dasman Palace, formerly the residence of Shaikh Ahmad Al-Jabir, is still used by members of the ruling family. Other structures of historical or architectural interest will be preserved but they can convey no impression of Kuwait as it was in the pre-oil era. The new and the old are dimensions apart.

Above: Ceremonial robes worn by this girl are richly embroidered and decorated with gold sequins. Left: A waiter in ceremonial dress stands in front of an old city door. He wears the traditional headdress *Ghatra*, with a black band, *Egu*. The strong bitter coffee is served in small cups

Nature's Bounty

Right: Wellhead maintenance in Rhawdatain

Oil is the lifeblood of Kuwait. Its discovery has transformed a small, regionally oriented Arab State into a financial colossus of universal fame. For millions of years Kuwait's massive treasure-house of oil and natural gas lay buried beneath a vast expanse of inhospitable desert steppes, unknown, unsought and unused. And then came the discovery of vast deposits in a world hungry for new energy sources—a discovery generating enormous wealth and making possible the transformation of an entire state. The story is fascinating. Black, oily substances on the surface of the sands have often been referred to in Arabic literature and travellers' tales. The Arab use of bitumen was extensive in many areas. In 1859, the first "strike" was made in the United States and, ten years later, oil was found in Egypt. In 1908, oil began to flow in Iran (then Persia) but it was not until thirty years later that Kuwait's underground wealth was finally tapped.

For several years, the "oil explorers" were roaming the wide expanse of the Gulf area: in Bahrain, Saudi Arabia, Iraq and elsewhere. In what is now Iran the Anglo-Persian Oil Company had successfully started an oil industry and, in other Gulf areas, there were high hopes that the black patches, well known in history, would yield similar results. There arrived on the Kuwait scene a New Zealander, Major Frank Holmes, a mining engineer who had been drilling water wells for the ruler, Shaikh Ahmad Al Jabir Al Sabah. He had seen black patches in the desert and he felt confident they presaged an abundant flow of oil on the Persian pattern. He travelled extensively prospecting and he asked for an oil and gas option just when the Anglo-Persian Oil Company's negotiator, Mr. A. H. Chisholm, arrived in Kuwait.

In 1933, the Gulf Oil Corporation of America made an arrangement with Major Holmes transferring his "moral rights" to them. Major Holmes represented Gulf during a long series of negotiations at a time when there was intense rivalry with Anglo-Persian. Finally, Gulf and Anglo-Persian (now British Petroleum) agreed to form a partnership and the Kuwait Oil Company Ltd. was formed in 1934 with the two companies as equal partners. The company was registered in London in view of British political predominance in the area at that time. A technical document dated June 1, 1935,

compiled by two geologists, Peter Cox and Ralph Rhoades, set the stage for the complete transformation of Kuwait's economy and its rise to international prominence.

Cox and Rhoades had been travelling to almost every part of the State in search of prospective and viable deposits. Gas seepages had been seen at Bahrah, north of Kuwait Bay, and the two men recommended that a well should be drilled there. The result was disappointing in that only a slow oil-seepage occurred which could not possibly be a commercial proposition. Despite this, they advised that particular attention should be paid to an area south of Kuwait Bay between Madenayat and Burgan which they believed might offer the possibility of oil deposits. Their advice was followed and a well was drilled at Burgan in company with others in the area.

A gusher was found. Under enormous pressure the oil burst through the well-head valve and a black spout soared high into the desert air. There was insufficient mud to block the drilling hole and a frantic search produced a 60-foot pole, found in Kuwait town, which was quickly sheared to the dimensions required and placed in the well-head as a temporary stopper. It did its job and Burgan Number One—still producing oil today—had been spudded in successfully. On what was a barren expanse of flat, sandy steppes extending in monotonous and inhospitable bleakness to the horizon, there rose on the foundation of that gusher at Burgan the town of Ahmadi, now the bustling headquarters of the Kuwait Oil Company, the country's largest producer and the backbone of the economy. Like modern Kuwait, Ahmadi was no more than twenty-five years old when it spread out to transform the desert landscape.

The Burgan find was followed by more drilling and this confirmed earlier hopes of extensive production, but the outbreak of World War II stopped the flow of supplies and manpower. Operations were suspended in 1942, the wells were plugged with cement and the prospecting camp at Magwa was abandoned. At the end of the war in 1945, there was a vast influx of oil-workers into Kuwait: from Abadan in Iran, from Texas, Britain, India and many other places. The Magwa camp was reactivated and an armada of equipment was assembled there—earthmovers, tractors, compressors, steel-work in all shapes and sizes. A mobile American war-time hospital was set up and a Scottish engineering company provided all the requirements of steel. Mr. C. A. P. (later Sir Philip) Southwell, after whom the KOC South-well Hospital (now the Ahmadi Hospital) was named, became managing director of the KOC. The aim of the BP-Gulf partnership was exports in 1946.

Conditions were harsh. The sun blazed down to test human stamina with temperatures reaching more than 45° Centigrade in the shade (if any could be found in that treeless expanse). The work-force was drawn from Kuwait and from regions beyond. The build-up saw 9,000 workers concentrated in what is now Ahmadi town and another 9,000 at scattered locations in Burgan, Magwa, Fahaheel and Shuwaikh—then mostly tent encampments—and in Kuwait town. The tents were followed by Nissen huts and these were augmented by Callow huts, so named from the initials of two engineers who found a method of building them from local materials. The building gangs, mostly from Britain, worked from October to April and then, finding the summer heat too much to bear, returned home until the cooler weather arrived again.

The first submarine pipeline was laid between Fahaheel and Shuaiba, now the site of a vast industrial area. From the sea, the site had the advantage of being at the end of a natural channel leading to deep water and the Gulf. On land, there was a ridge across the pipeline route from Burgan some 400 feet above sea level. It was on that ridge that the town of Ahmadi was built. The ridge acted as a natural wind-break to defy the ubiquitous sandstorms and there was a gentle slope to the sea allowing the oil to flow under gravity. This facilitated sewage disposal and water drainage. The humidity at the coast was reduced by the rise of the land and its easy drainage position.

There was no air-conditioning and in Kuwait's torrid summers salt loss from the body became a serious problem, solved only by the import of huge quantities of salt from several overseas sources. Water, too, was a precious commodity. A fleet of five ships carrying 50,000 tons carried fresh water from the Shatt Al Arab. As many as 49 voyages were made every month. Earlier—in 1940—the discovery of a reservoir of brackish water at Burgan had eased the shortage of water for industrial use. More brackish water was found during drilling operations at Manageesh and in 1942 another reservoir was tapped at Adeliyah. The water was used for making the "mud" essential for drilling operations. The first brackish water field developed to supply Kuwait town, about 40 kilometres from the Ahmadi site, was found at Sleibiyah in 1941. It was an abundant source and production reached 20 million gallons a day.

As the outline of Ahmadi gradually took shape, the KOC developed its own brackish water system from Adeliyah. Pipelines were laid to the

Overleaf: A typical oil storage farm on the edge of the desert

63

embryo town and a network was built to connect the supply to offices, houses, clubs and other buildings. Later another pipeline connected the supply to the government's distillation plant which was built at Shuaiba. As Kuwait developed its own water resources this supply was replaced by water from other reservoirs.

In 1946, the first sea-loading line was built and in June that year the first cargo of crude oil was exported from Kuwait. The construction of a pier (the South Pier) had been started. Work was proceeding on what was to become a 4,000-tons-a-day refinery, a power station and a sea-water distillation plant. Ahmadi was taking the shape it has today. New drilling rigs were at work over a scattered area. Road graders were pushing over the desert. An aeroplane—a de Havilland *Rapide* biplane—flew from a hard sandy strip on

Right: A Kuwait Oil
Company wellhead.
Above right: A view of the
Kuwait Oil Company's
Ahmadi refinery

66

which had been placed its "tin" hangar. Nearby, a Nissen hut accommodated pilots and ground engineers.

Materials poured in and the tents and huts were replaced by permanent buildings. An ice-plant was working at full speed to produce 20 tons a day. A soda water factory arrived and then company canteens began to operate and retail stores were set up. Soon there was a large laundry with dry-cleaning facilities. The headquarters, which had been placed at Magwa, were moved to Ahmadi where a hospital was built. Streets were surfaced, power lines erected and a lone "lantana tree" was brought in by a visiting football team from Basra. It was planted and stood alone in the barren void of desert. Today it is one of many hundreds planted in a well planned urban area where grass, flowers, shrubs and trees flourish with ample supplies of brackish water. More than 1,000 homes had been built in 1952. Traffic flowed on newly paved streets. Sewage and gas systems had been installed. Gardens were planted and social activities organised.

In 1960, drilling operations by the KOC produced an event of momentous significance—the discovery of Kuwait's first fresh-water reservoir at Rhawdatain where construction work was proceeding on the Kuwait-Basra highway. The contractors were drilling for brackish water needed to mix concrete and for other purposes. The drilling began, a strike was made and water began to gush to the surface in great volume. There were scenes of great jubilation when it was found it was fresh—one of the greatest events in the history of a State which had formerly to rely on a few wells and supplies from the Shatt Al Arab. The Rhawdatain field, some 12 kilometres in length and about 5 kilometres wide, is a vast natural reservoir formed by rain water which had collected there for thousands of years. It has a capacity of 5 million gallons a day and a lifespan at that production level of 25 years. Production, however, was pegged at 3 million gallons and, wisely, the government took other measures to conserve the supply. These included the construction of an open tank to collect rain water which is fed to the natural reservoir through a canal system.

Ahmadi by the 1960s was a full-sized township complete with guest-house, blocks of bachelor flats, and a shopping centre with supermarkets and a cinema. There were 76 miles of tarmac roads, a water-storage capacity of about 19 million gallons and a conglomeration of workshops, stores, re-frigeration plants, air conditioned buildings and office complexes. The township is a haven of quietness compared with the ceaseless roar of traffic

Nature's Bounty

in the capital city. Its buildings are on a lesser scale. There is greenery everywhere and the comparative solitude of a rural existence. Yet it is the focal point of Kuwait's wealth, the headquarters of the country's biggest money-earner. Round and about are the signs of its importance: the rigs, the storage containers, the pipelines, the refinery . . . all the metal work of an industry vital to the well-being of every member of the population.

While the Kuwait Oil Company concession was by far the biggest and the most productive, other areas were exploited by various groups in search of crude-oil sources. In 1946, the Wafra concession in the Kuwait-Saudi Arabian divided, or Neutral, zone, where the countries shared equal rights, was granted to the American Independent Oil Company (Aminoil). The Saudi Arabian rights went to the Getty Oil Company. Oil was struck at Wafra in 1953 and the first full year saw a production of 2.8 million barrels compared with 509.4 million barrels from KOC fields. In 1958 the Getty company completed a refinery with a capacity of 50,000 barrels a day at Mena Saud in the divided zone and Aminoil built a 30,000-barrel refinery at Mena Abdullah in Kuwait. Marine exploration rights off the divided zone, outside territorial

Below: An oil storage farm on the edge of the sea from which oil tankers are supplied. Above right and overleaf: The flaring of natural gas, a sight which will soon vanish from the Kuwaiti landscape with the advent of a new natural gas project. Below right: The Sea Island—a pier for loading oil into supertankers

Above: An oil refinery of the Kuwait National Petroleum Company in the Shuaiba Industrial Area. Above and below left: Oil refineries

waters, were granted to the Japanese-owned Arabian Oil Company in 1958 by agreement between Kuwait and Saudi Arabia. Each country signed separate contracts with AOC and both countries took up a 10 per cent shareholding in the company.

A new submarine field was found at Khafji and by May 1961, 14 wells were producing 6,000 barrels a day. By 1969, production had reached more than 16.5 million tons.

In 1961, Shaikh Abdullah concluded a 45-year agreement with the Kuwait Shell Petroleum Development Company Limited, to explore for oil in an area including the sea-bed and sub-soil in the Arabian Gulf from the coast over a distance of 6 nautical miles. Pending the settlement of border questions no exploration activities were carried out by Kuwait Shell after 1964. In 1960, the Kuwait National Petroleum Company (KNPC) was incorporated with a capital of KD. 7.5 million (60 per cent held by government and 40 per cent by private Kuwaiti shareholders) to market a part of the KOC's refinery products locally—gasoline, kerosene, gas, oil and bitumen. The KNPC now markets world-wide.

When in May 1962, the KOC relinquished about 9,262 square kilometres of its concession to the government, the KNPC was granted the right to explore for and exploit any oil that might be found in the surrendered area. The KNPC chose a Spanish Company, Hispanica de Petroleos (HISPANOIL) to share with it the development of the concession on the basis of 51 per cent for KNPC and 49 per cent for Hispanoil. A joint operation company, the Kuwait Spanish Petroleum Company, was formed in 1968 to start work in the concession area. Already by the middle of 1965, the KNPC had started to build a refinery at Shuaiba and this was completed in 1968. The refinery, the largest in the world to operate with hydrogen in all its units, has a capacity of nearly 100,000 barrels a day.

The KNPC later took over an 80 per cent shareholding in the Kuwait Aviation Fuelling Company (KAFCO). This company supplies all aircraft with necessary fuels such as kerosene, gasoline and some of the special lubricants. KNPC supplies aviation turbine kerosene.

Kuwait was among the founding members of both the Organisation of Petroleum Exporting Countries (OPEC) and the Organisation of Arab Petroleum Exporting Countries (OAPEC). It also participates in all the works of the petroleum committees and conferences of the League of Arab States.

Kuwaitisation

Oil today has become a vital issue in world affairs and its importance to the well-being of every country needs no elaboration. The world is hungry for oil as the major source of energy and this dependence has greatly increased the importance of the role played by the producing countries, prominent among them Kuwait. It is now apparent that the predominant part played by the major oil companies up to recent years in exploiting and marketing the crude oil of the producing countries has been greatly reduced by the determination of the producers, particularly the Arab states, to take full control of their own natural resources for the greater benefit of their peoples. Thus, in the Arabian Gulf in particular, the oil industry is undergoing a rapid process of change and the picture that will emerge will reflect, in Kuwait as elsewhere, the inflexible resolve of the owners of these gigantic resources to control them and to exploit them for the national interest, with the prosperity of future generations chiefly in mind.

In March 1975, Kuwait announced its intention to take over its major oil producer, the Kuwait Oil Company. Almost 12 months earlier, a participation agreement was signed to give the Kuwait Government 60 per cent control of the KOC with the remaining 40 per cent shareholding being equally divided between British Petroleum and Gulf Oil, the former co-owners of the company with a 50 per cent stake each. The 1975 takeover, which gave Kuwait 100 per cent ownership of the company, was a logical extension of the government-backed policy of Kuwaitisation, which has been laid down as a major programme since operations started—a process intended to place Kuwait's own natural resources in Kuwaiti hands. This has been accelerated year after year as new generations of citizens, all of them highly equipped educationally, have acquired the necessary technical and administrative skills to occupy top executive positions in the company.

In the KOC—the country's prime asset—Kuwaitis today are the largest single nationality group, forming half the work-force. Recruitment of university graduates and secondary-school leavers and the extensive training facilities provided by the company have made it the second largest employer of Kuwaitis after the government. From the day of the first successful drilling at Burgan the KOC record has been one of rapid expansion. In 1958, the refinery input was 190,000 barrels a day and, in 1959, the export capacity reached more than 2 million barrels a day. New targets continued to be reached. In 1964, crude oil production and exports in a single year exceeded 100 million tons. In 1965, the 1,000 millionth barrel of oil was produced. In 1970, the KOC refinery produced the billionth barrel of refined product. A new annual record was achieved in 1972, with a production of 148,711,076 long tons. In line with government policy, production is now regulated to an annual ceiling officially fixed.

From 1946 to 1953, the KOC produced 1,077,291,000 barrels of crude and from 1954 to 1960 the total reached 3,170,249,000 barrels. In 1961, the production was 600,226,000 barrels increasing annually to a 1973 total of 1,004,781,000 barrels. The Arabian Oil Company production rose from 3,551,000 barrels in 1961 to 71,912,000 barrels in 1973. The Aminoil production reached 25,772,000 barrels in 1973 compared with 29,284,000 in 1961. Thus, the total production reached 155,746,000 tons in 1973 (1,102,465,000 barrels). Exports showed similar expansion. In 1957, Kuwait exported 54,910,000 tons of crude and 2,403,000 tons of refined products. In 1973, crude oil exports totalled 131,114,000 tons and refined products 19,385,000 tons.

Natural gas, too, played an important part in Kuwait's economy. This is a co-product of the crude-oil production process. The natural reservoir energy which thrusts the oil out of the ground is partly due to the amount of this volatile gas in the crude. Since the late 1940s, gas has been used to power the turbine generators at the power stations and the sea-water distillation plants. Not all the natural gas can be used. However, in 1959, KOC started a gas-injection programme by which a gas-injection plant at Burgan compressed and injected up to 100 million cubic feet of gas a day back into producing formations in the oilfield. This helps to maintain reservoir pressure and conserves the gas. Later, two similar plants were put into operation.

Increases in the posted price of oil agreed by the member States of OPEC and new trends in the international oil market following the assumption of increased control of their oil industries by the producing countries have changed production trends everywhere. The days of maximum production would seem to have disappeared, a prime reason for this being the desire of the producers to increase their underground reserve capacity. In addition, by the beginning of 1975 international demand for crude oil had been decreased by an energy-conservation drive and the piling up of reserve stocks.

Thus, in February 1975, what was then Kuwait's Ministry of Finance and Oil announced a daily production average during the previous month of 2,036,139 barrels. The month's total reached 63,120,392 barrels compared with 87,963,363 in the corresponding month in 1974—a decrease of 28.24 per cent. The company production figures for January 1975 were: 56,008,105 (1,806,713 daily) barrels compared with 79,965,874 barrels in January 1974—a decrease of 29.96 per cent; Aminoil: 2,856,789 barrels compared with 1,846,203 barrels in January, 1974—an increase of 54.75 per cent; The Arabian Oil Company (Japan): 4,255,408 barrels compared with 6,151,296 in January, 1974—a decrease of 30.82 per cent.

According to OPEC statistics, Kuwait's production cut in 1974 was in line with the general trend towards oil conservation by producing countries. During the year, Kuwait had the second biggest production cut of member states of 15.7 per cent. The largest was that of Libya where production fell in 1974 by 30.3 per cent. The overall production of OPEC States reached 30,838,000 barrels a day in 1974 which was 0.5 per cent lower than in 1973.

In 1973, Kuwait was the third largest exporter of oil behind Saudi Arabia and Iran. The totals were: Saudi Arabia 351 million tons, Iran 264 million, Kuwait 132 million, Libya 109 million, Venezuela 106 million, USSR 103 million, Nigeria 99 million, Abu Dhabi 65 million and Indonesia 51 million. By far the biggest importer, as in previous years, for Kuwait's oil was Japan which received from various sources a total of 230 million tons of oil. Other top importers were the USA (162 million tons), France (136 million), Italy (126 million), Britain (115 million) and the Federal Republic of Germany (11 million).

A significant move in the general context of Kuwait's oil affairs took place in 1975 when the Ministry of Finance and Oil was divided and two ministries created: that of Finance under a Minister and a new Ministry of Oil. Earlier, there had been the formation of the Kuwait Oil, Gas and Energy Corporation, a private shareholding concern with the participation of the Kuwait Petrochemical Company, the Kuwait National Petroleum Company and the Kuwait Foreign Trading, Contracting and Investment Company. The company, with an initial capital of KD. 150 million, was formed to deal with all oil and natural resources matters in the State after ratification of the Participation Agreement with KOC. It has been charged, in an Amiri Decree, with managing all aspects of the oil industry in Kuwait pending the formation of a government body to take over the industry.

While early in 1975 the entire oil industry in the Gulf region was in the process of undergoing extensive changes, it was apparent in Kuwait that the preservation of underground reserves was considered, as elsewhere, to be of paramount importance. Thus, in 1975, the average daily production ceiling was fixed at an average of 2,000,000 barrels—a reduction from the previous average of about 500,000 barrels a day. This left the State with the capacity to augment reserves by vast amounts, a step that received unanimous welcome in the National Assembly. For Kuwait—and possibly for other regions in the Gulf—the prospect exists for further sources of oil to be found. In particular, the neutral zone has shown promise of new deposits of both oil and natural gas. Surveys are continuing both on land and offshore.

Natural gas will assume a prominent role in the future. The amount consumed in 1973 was estimated to be about 48 per cent of production. This rose to 50 per cent in 1974. Under a new project, the initial cost of which was estimated at KD. 30 million, a plant will be constructed to liquefy five million metric tons of natural gas annually. In addition, a fleet of 15 tankers will be built for exporting the gas at an estimated cost of US $500 million. Liquid petroleum gas exports in 1973 totalled 21,352,012 barrels.

Vibrant Energy

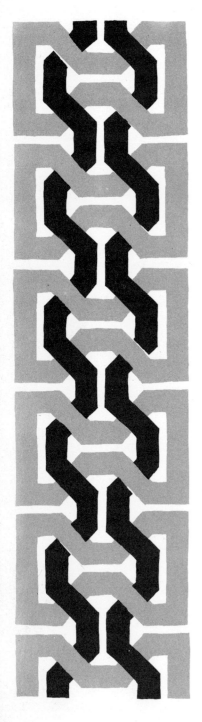

Oil and natural gas, on which the country's prosperity has been founded, provide the energy for Kuwait's massive sea water distillation plants and the power stations which today perform a service most vital to the life of every inhabitant. Electricity in its many forms is a world-wide possession and it arouses little interest. Kuwait, no less than the other capital cities of the world, runs on electricity. Yet, by comparison, its evolution from oil lamps to power stations has leapt over the slow progression of the large industrial countries in a staggering build up of energy unleashed by the discovery of oil and gas.

Similar—and even more remarkable—has been the advance made in sea water distillation efficiency. Kuwait has become a world consultant in distillation techniques. The modern marvel of an abundant supply of fresh water from the State's unlimited asset, the sea, has drawn the attention of many nations to dwindling fresh water supplies in the wake of the population explosion, rapid industrial growth and the menace of pollution in natural reserves of mankind's vital life-source.

The technological triumph over its almost waterless past has been achieved in an amazingly short space of time—almost overnight in the context of comparative development elsewhere—and at great cost. The industrial nations, faced with the threat of expanding populations and extensive industrial growth, have looked to Kuwait for technical advice. Two American cities, San Francisco and New York, have made studies of Kuwait's sea water distillation complex. Britain has sought advice. More recently, Hong Kong, planning to build a desalination plant, sent its engineers to Kuwait. Several other countries have been provided with information garnered from Kuwait's vast experience and knowledge of sea water distillation.

The sea is Kuwait's unlimited storehouse of raw material to provide both electricity and potable water. Natural gas provides the energy and an amazing complex of intricate machinery in increasing activity uses both to produce the brilliance, the power and the progress of modern Kuwait. The two sources of power generation are located at Shuwaikh and Shuaiba where the plants are co-ordinated so that part of the boiler steam is used for power generation and the other part for water distillation. Natural gas from the oilfield nearby is the producer of heat.

Both sea water distillation and power generation have been developed to their present state of engineering excellence by the Ministry of Electricity and Water, which has brought an era of vibrant energy sources into an area of desert, a region with no rivers and an annual rainfall that varies between a half and fourteen inches of rain a year. Daily commerce, industry and life itself are dependent on the electricity and water supplies provided by the Ministry, which, over the past two decades, has grown from a tiny department to one of the largest government employers. Its achievements have been no less remarkable than that of Kuwait's transformation from "Little Fort" to space-age metropolis.

The story of electricity, like that of water, has been a record of accelerated demand—of 20-year plans for expansion being out-dated by domestic needs within 3 years. The more power generated the more was used. Supply could hardly keep pace with demand but the Ministry has performed a herculean task in matching output with the prodigious climb in consumption. All this provides the staggering contrast between present and the recent past when Kuwait was a small walled town with a population of about 60,000 in the 1930s. Those were the days of kerosene lamps, of mud brick buildings and narrow, meandering streets. Nevertheless, there was electricity—provided by small generators for some limited use.

In 1934, the first supply of electricity reached private consumers. It was provided by a privately owned generating plant driven by a horizontal single cylinder oil engine. In the next five years, the output of the plant was increased tenfold but the outbreak of World War II stopped expansion because the Kuwaiti merchants, who owned the generators, were unable to buy new equipment. After the war, the company sought specialised advice and, in 1949, two new 200-kilowatt generators were bought and put in commission in the powerhouse at Mergab, situated within the town's wall. These machines provided alternating current and in 1950, the entire direct current distribution system was converted to alternating current. The old plant was closed down.

Later, more machinery was installed to bring a total of 930 kilowatts of plant into commission by 1951. It was ample then but, only twelve years later, the growth of demand made its output seem puny—an increase by more than

Overleaf left: A general view of Kuwait City at night. Overleaf right: One of Kuwait's modern Mosques, constructed on traditional Islamic architectural principles

a hundred times to 100 megawatts. A massive development programme was under way. To this was added the improved standard of living Kuwaitis had come to expect and this included air-conditioning in a climate of summer temperatures often exceeding 45° Centigrade in the shade. Then, as now, the biggest individual peak-hour consumer was the air-conditioner. In 1951, the old Department of Electricity was founded to take over the task of meeting demand. New and second-hand generators were bought and quickly commissioned. Still a major expansion of plants was necessary.

In 1952, the first power station designed for the use of thermal energy from steam was built. It consisted of three small steam turbines of back-pressure type to run three A.C. generators of 750 kW each. Superheated steam used for the turbines was produced from three tube boilers and steam generated from the boilers was partially used for the steam turbines. The remainder went to heat up sea water in Kuwait's first distillation plant. The site was Shuwaikh, close to the harbour and the source of sea water needed for the condensers in the steam turbo-generating system. Water and electricity existed side by side, interdependent and vital for the livelihood of the people.

The demand for electricity increased by leaps and bounds. What became known as "A" power station was in full generation by 1955—four turbo-alternators of 7,500 kW each. The station was designed to pass out its steam for use in a second distillation plant—the "B" water distillation station. Still the demand for electricity increased at the exceptional rate of more than 25 per cent annually. It became imperative to expand the generating power at Shuwaikh. "B" and "C" power stations were built with respective capacities of 40,000 and 90,000 kW to bring the installed output of all the power stations to 166,500 kW—a tremendous increase over the 1951 figure of 930 kW. By 1962, the demand had increased by 38.4 per cent, way beyond the wildest guess of the Ministry experts. Statistics vividly reveal the scope of the rocketing demand: in 1951 there were 2,462 consumers, in 1952 the number had doubled to 5,067, in 1953 there were 8,747 and, in one year, another 4,401 consumers were connected to bring the total to 13,148. By 1955, there were 16,046 consumers using more than 58 million kWh. Two more years added 50 per cent to the number of consumers—bringing it up to 25,023. The number of units consumed was nearly 119 million.

A new 11,000 volt distribution network had been introduced and the first 11,000 volt underground cable was laid from the Mergab diesel power station to a sub-station near the old Jahra Gate to supply a densely populated area of the town. Overhead lines carrying 11,000 volts were installed and these were later converted to underground cables as building activity increased. The four new 10,000 kW. generators in "B" power station generated at 11,000 volts, like the others, but were fed into a newly commissioned 33,000-volt distribution system through large transformers. This system was developed to meet the needs of what were then remote domestic areas. Sub-stations stepped down the voltage to 11,000 with a further reduction to give a three-phase low-tension supply for domestic use.

In 1958, "C" power station was constructed. This comprised three much larger generators of 30,000 kilowatts each. In 1961, the department became a ministry and the first of the three 30,000 kW units was commissioned. In 1962, with the other two units installed the State's total government supply capacity rose to 160,000 kilowatts. Yet still the capacity was insufficient. By 1965, a new industrial expansion programme was started at Shuaiba, about 45 kilometres from Kuwait City, and Shuaiba North power station with three 70,000 kilowatt generators was commissioned. From 1957 to 1962, annual consumption rose from 119 million to 418 million kWh. By 1967, the figure had reached 1.3 thousand million units. Of this total only 117 million kWh was used by industrial plants. The remainder was consumed by a population with almost universal use of cars, refrigerators, air-conditioners, radios, and television sets. The Ministry set up an air-conditioning department and the first government building to have air-conditioning was the Amiri hospital on the sea front; a 25-ton unit was placed in the operating theatre in 1953.

In the Shuwaikh power station the total capacity of steam turbo-alternators is 160,000 kilowatts. At Shuaiba North the total capacity is 400,000 kilowatts. The adjoining Shuaiba South power station, completed in 1972, has a capcity of 536,000 kilowatts. Overall capacity was 1,096,000 kilowatts (1,096 mega-watts). Still, this was not enough. Two more 134,000 kilowatt units are in operation at Shuaiba South to produce 804,000 kilowatts and in 1974 the capacity overall reached 1,364,000 kilowatts (1,364 megawatts). The main transmission today is 132 kV with sub-transmission and distribution at 33 kV and 11 kV. There is a widespread network of 132 kV overhead lines, of under-ground cables, sub-stations and a massive network of lines to bring the brilliance of modern living.

An average of from four to eight 132 kV sub-stations are being built annually. About the same number of 33 kV sub-stations go up each year and approximately 159 kV sub-stations are built in a twelve-month period. On average, between ten and thirty kilometres of 132 kV underground cables are laid. Between twenty to thirty kilometres of 33 kV cables are laid and for 11 kV cables the average is about 150 kilometres. In 1956, not one 132 kV sub-station existed. There was one in 1964. At the end of 1974 there were seventeen. In 1964, there were 33 11 kV sub-stations. In 1974 there were 45 in operation. From a nil figure in 1956, overhead transmission lines operating at 132 kV reached 48.5 kilometres by 1964 and increased during the next ten years to 356.7 kilometres. There were 25 kilometres of 33 kV overhead lines in 1956. These totalled 427.8 kilometres in 1974. In 1956 there was a nil figure for 132 kV underground cables; in 1965 a total of 4.3 kilometres; in 1974 no less than 70 kilometres. In 1956, there were 25 kilometres of 33 kV underground cables. By the end of 1974 this had grown to 374.7 kilometres. The peak load in 1956 was 21 megawatts. In 1974 it was 975 megawatts.

Street lighting has seen a continuous expansion from a total of 1,632 low mast and high mast poles in 1956 to 38,611 at the end of 1974. There were 100 kilometres of streets and carriage-ways served by street lighting in 1956. In 1974, the total was 1,293 kilometres. The meteoric rise in Kuwait's consumer demand seems likely to continue in the forseeable future and, certainly up to 1980, the guidelines have been set to meet every contingency. At Doha, about 30 kilometres from Kuwait City, and at Shuwaikh power and water plants were under construction in 1974. The major project at Doha envisages a plant of four units with a possible extension to seven. Each unit will have a capacity of 150 MW with the first unit scheduled for operation in January 1977. Doha is expected to be fully operational in January 1978.

At Shuwaikh there will be five new gas-turbine units each of 40.8 MW to give a total of 204 MW. The first unit is due to go into operation in January 1976 and the others at one month intervals thereafter. The addition of the new power stations will give a total capacity of about 2,168 MW but this can be increased by the expansion of the Doha units to seven. By 1979 and 1980, the total capacity will reach 2,618 MW. By contrast with the other stations, the Doha plant has been designed to fire any of four kinds of fuel: natural gas, tail gas from the proposed LPG plant, gas-oil and crude oil. The others remain on gas and oil. A project of special interest is the supply of electricity and water to Failaka Island by means of submarine cables and pipeline. This will replace both the diesel powerhouse and the tankers which now ferry the island's water supply. The project is expected to be in commission by 1977 when Failaka will have been developed as a resort.

Abundant Streams

From the earliest days of civilisation water has been the problem of the arid countries of Arabia. In Kuwait there is no bounty of river water. There are no lakes. For generation after generation Kuwaitis knew only the scant security of a few underground wells. The wells and their life-giving water were the basis of Arab life for centuries. It is almost inconceivable that Kuwait today, with an abundant supply of water for every purpose provided by its giant distillation system, its underground fresh water reservoir at Rhawdatain and its brackish water reserves, was at the turn of the century dependent on a few wells. Water was then a scarce and valuable commodity. The story of Kuwait's unparalleled upsurge to complete self-sufficiency in water is similar to that of the electricity saga—a tribute to an administration which used the new oil riches to enhance the well-being of the population and change the poorly endowed past to the abundant present with its treasury of amenities, all within a few years.

Kuwait contains brackish water lying at a few hundred feet below the surface. The water is almost ten times as salty as acceptable drinking water or sweet water. It is, however, ten times less salty than sea water. In the old days the main sources of fresh water were scattered sweet-water wells and water imported from the Shatt-al-Arab river in Iraq. Dhows used to sail from the river down to Kuwait laden with the precious water which was sold to motorised or donkey-carriers for distribution. Then the goatskin bag was an essential article of everyday life.

So rapid was the transformation from the age of wells and dhows that Kuwaitis in their late twenties or early thirties can remember the scene during their childhood—the carriers, the men with the long poles over their shoulders carrying the water containers slung at each end of the poles. Water was stored in large, cemented holes dug in the ground or in large earthenware containers. Donkeys carried the water to the houses. Today those young men and women merely turn on a tap and the water flows. They have the latest bathrooms and showers. There is an abundant supply throughout the State. With such vast quantities of fresh water being produced from both natural and artificial sources memories grow dim and the age of the

Above: Kuwait is now abundantly supplied with water from its sea water distillation plants; formerly Kuwaitis had to rely on a few scattered wells such as this one. Right: The Shuwaikh water distillation plant, the first to be built in Kuwait

dhow-borne water and the carriers will soon be relegated to the pages of history.

Nevertheless, with a much smaller population, the old town was well served by wells. Several fresh-water wells at Shamiya, outside the wall, provided much of the drinking water. Another group of wells in the western part of the town was discovered and these helped to maintain an adequate supply. In 1905, the Hawalli well was found. It was a momentous event and sons born that year were named Hawalli; dhows launched at the time were given the name. Its only drawback was its vulnerability in less peaceful

times. It was outside the wall and all water drawn from the well had to be carried some distance to homes within the town wall.

In 1925, a seafarer, Sultan bin Mahmoud, placed several empty barrels in the hold of a dhow and sailed to the Shatt-Al-Arab. He returned with the barrels filled with fresh water and berthed at a jetty near Shuwaikh. The water was emptied into a small reservoir and was then sold. Within six months many dhows had been converted for water-carrying by the installation of tanks. In 1939, a company was formed to run a fleet and three large reservoirs were built on the shore of the Bay of Kuwait for water to be pumped into them from the dhow tanks. The dhows each carried up to 8,500 gallons. By 1946 there were thirty-five dhows on the run. The Kuwait Oil Company was supplied with Shatt-Al-Arab water and in the peak year of 1947 about 80,000 gallons were reaching Kuwait daily. Finally, the trade disappeared as suddenly as it had arrived. Its purpose was defeated by the construction of the KOC sea water distillation plant at Mena Al-Ahmadi and, in 1951, the dhows pumped their water into the reservoirs for the last time.

At first the oil company's distillation plant had piped 80,000 gallons a day to Kuwait but the Department of Electricity of the time had ordered its first distillation complex on the Shuwaikh site and when this was commissioned in 1953 the KOC ceased to supply Kuwait. At first the Shuwaikh plant sent its water to two three-million-gallon reservoirs about a mile away. Then brackish water to replace the minerals lost was added to the distilled water at the Shuwaikh pumping station, but now it is pumped straight into the reservoirs.

At the end of 1953, Kuwait drinking water was chlorinated for the first time and chlorine production was started in the State in 1963. Other additives to the water were fifteen parts per million of lime and ten parts per million of sodium bicarbonate. The amount of chlorine was two parts per million. The water was pumped to four 160,000-gallon tanks held 115 feet above sea level. These tanks fed the four lorry-filling stations which carried the water to consumers. The tanks have now been replaced by architecturally pleasing water towers. The controlled supply of brackish water began in 1953 with the opening of eight wells. A three-million gallon reservoir was built and finished late in 1953 near the Shuwaikh fresh water reservoirs.

By 1962 80 wells had been commissioned within a 12-mile radius of Kuwait City and in 1963 another 25 were commissioned. In the summer of 1960, a scheme was started to provide a supply of piped brackish water. By early 1963 about 5,000 customers had been connected to the main. The main domestic uses are for watering trees and general household purposes. In 1962, drinking water consumption broke all records. On June 10, no less than 7,557,000 gallons were supplied at the Ministry's filling stations. The record did not stand for long. Each year has seen new heights reached in the supply and consumption of water. Statistics again tell the story. In 1954 some 259 million gallons of potable water were produced. Ten years later the figure was 2,200 million and in 1967 it reached 4,200 million. The State was also able to supply 12 million gallons a day and by the late 1960s the sea was giving up around 23 million gallons a day of fresh water, largely for domestic consumption.

Nearly ten years after the commissioning of the first Shuwaikh distillation plant the sweet water reservoir at Rhawdatain was discovered during road-building operations. By 1962 it was providing 2 million gallons a day; a welcome addition to the State's distilled water supply.

With the establishment of ten industrial concerns at Shuaiba intakes were erected to supply sea water for cooling purposes to the industries. Among the plants were the Shuaiba North and South power and water distillation stations which served all the industries with distilled water. Today Shuwaikh's water distillation plants consist of a number of multi-stage flash type distillation units with a total capacity of 18 million gallons of distilled water daily. They are:

"A" (new) plant comprising one unit with a total capacity of 4 million imperial gallons a day. Commissioned in 1970.

'B' (new plant) comprising two units with a capacity of 2 million gallons a day. Commissioned in 1968.

"C" and "D" plants comprising four units each with a capacity of half a million gallons a day. Total capacity 2 million gallons. Commissioned in 1957 and 1958.

"E" plant. Two units of 1 million gallon capacity. Total capacity 2 million gallons. Commissioned in 1960.

"F" plant. Two units of 1 million gallon capacity. Total capacity 2 million gallons. Commissioned in 1965.

"G" plant. Two units of 2 million gallon capacity. Total capacity 4 million gallons. Commissioned in 1968.

Total daily capacity: 18 million gallons.

Abundant Streams   The capital cost of the entire distillation system was Kuwaiti Dinars 9,000,000 (about US $31 million). By far the largest complex is situated at Shuaiba where the North plant has a capacity of 14 million gallons a day and the more recent South plant 20 million gallons. This has been increased to 30 million gallons with the installation of two new units. Total capacity is 62 million gallons daily. The North Plant comprises:

"A" plant. Three units of 1 million gallons. Total capacity 3 million gallons a day. All commissioned 1965–66.

"B" plant. One unit of 2 million gallons. Commissioned in 1968.

"C" plant. Two units of 2 million gallons. Total capacity 4 million gallons. Commissioned in 1968.

"D" plant. One unit of 5 million gallons. Commissioned in 1971.

The South plant comprises four huge multi-stage flash type units with a total capacity of 20 million gallons a day. The addition of two similar units has brought production capacity to 30 million gallons.

A valuable addition to Kuwait's distillation plants came in the form of an electrolytic chlorine caustic soda plant built by the Ministry to ensure regular supplies of chlorine. Another by-product is salt which is produced from concentrated sea water discharged from the distillation plants by triple-effect evaporator. Part of the production is conveyed to the electrolytic chlorine caustic plant. Free-flowing table salt is packed for sale and large quantities of commodity salt, packed in sacks, are also produced.

In less than thirty years—one generation—Kuwait has become self-sufficient in water for human consumption and industrial use. The cost has been enormous. At the end of 1973–74 the total bill was around KD. 100 million (more than $330 million). In power generation the Ministry invested KD. 133,540,000 (about $460 million). Brackish water fields and the natural reservoir of fresh water at Rhawdatain have played an important part in supplying ever-increasing demand. Storage capacity for water is now between 80 million and 100 million gallons.

Situated on the foreshore of Kuwait Bay are three towers of futuristic design. They are already a landmark to travellers arriving by air, sea or land routes. These towers have been designed to perform two functions: to augment the country's supply of fresh water and to provide attractive facilities for recreational pursuits. The towers are designed as a group of three units of white painted circular columns of concrete. The tallest one—180 metres high—supports two spheres, the larger and lower of which contains a water

reservoir while an elegant restaurant and garden occupy the upper half. On the upper sphere there is a cafeteria and a revolving viewing platform. The second tower—140 metres high—supports one sphere containing a water reservoir. They are floodlit from the third column. Each reservoir has a capacity of almost 1 million gallons and is only part of a vast expansion programme. They will join a total of 31 mushroom towers, each of which has a capacity of almost 660,000 gallons. By 1980, Kuwait will be using two fields of brackish water, there will be extensions to all pumping stations and up to 52 towers will dominate the flat landscape. Another project at Doha will be producing 40 million gallons a day of fresh water. Brackish water production will rise to about 88 million gallons a day with plenty in reserve.

Above: A view of the Shuwaikh water distillation plant and power complex

Diversification

The year 1974 marked the tenth anniversary of the establishment in Kuwait of the Shuaiba Area Authority, a vast industrial complex that has, among other achievements, produced the essential services which have given the people of the State one of the highest living standards in the world. Just over a decade ago Shuaiba was a barren stretch of land 50 kilometres south of Kuwait City. Today it accommodates a spread of industries that were founded on oil-wealth and which have successfully produced diversification of enterprises to change to some extent the image of Kuwait as a one-industry country. Shuaiba has established itself as a vital force in the country's progress. It is still expanding and the promise it holds for the future is auspicious.

In 1964, an area of about 8.4 million square metres south of the village of Shuaiba was chosen as the site of an industrial complex in Kuwait. There were many reasons for the choice, the most important of which were the depth of coastal water there, which reduced the cost of building harbour installations and the proximity of the source of materials and energy, crude oil and natural gas. On May 14 that year, an Amiri decree established the Shuaiba Industrial Development Board under the control of the Ministry of Finance and Industry. In 1970, another Amiri decree replaced the Board by the Shuaiba Area Authority which came under the control of the Ministry of Finance and Oil. Today more than 60 per cent of the area has been converted to industrial use and ten large enterprises manufacture a variety of products for domestic needs and export. In addition, the United Fisheries of Kuwait occupies an area of nearly 10,000 square metres with harbour installations for its fleet of more than 150 vessels.

Oil and gas have made Shuaiba a viable project but without another essential ingredient—water—there could have been no hope of ever getting off the ground. In co-operation with the Ministry of Electricity and Water the Authority made a start on using sea water, for cooling and distillation purposes. Early in 1967, the first intake was completed to serve the Shuaiba North power-and-water production station, the Kuwait National Petroleum

Company and the Kuwait Chemical Fertiliser Company. The second stage, completed in 1971, supplied the Shuaiba South power-and-water production station and the Petrochemical Industries Company. A third pumping station was later built to supply other industries. Cathodic protection and chlorination are used to treat the sea water and eliminate marine growth. In 1973, the consumption of sea water totalled 1,410 million cubic metres.

The Authority built a network of roads and drainage systems, street lighting and other services were provided and, to ensure safety and security within the area, police services have been established and there is a fully equipped fire-fighting station. Natural gas, as the energy source, was pumped from the Kuwait Oil Company's Burgan field gas-gathering centre through two pipelines. Construction of the Shuaiba harbour facilities started in 1964 and was completed in 1967 to provide a commercial harbour with the capacity to handle 1 million tons, a barge harbour for small craft, including fishing boats, and an oil pier for the loading of liquid petroleum products and liquid ammonia. The pier has two 45-foot deep berths and can accommodate tankers up to 100,000 DWT. Plans have been drawn up to extend the harbour works.

One of the main objects of the establishment of the area was to reduce the cost of importing raw materials and of exporting finished products from the industries. That was made possible by the building of the commercial harbour and oil pier. In addition, the provision of natural gas and cooling water from the sea assured the use of cheap materials with the bonus of economically priced electricity, distilled and fresh water services. A major aim of the Authority was to provide avenues of employment for Kuwaitis and to promote an industrial consciousness in the State. Since 1965, the number of Kuwaitis employed in the area has grown considerably, rising from 32 to more than 500 today.

On the economic side there have been the inevitable setbacks and problems of a trial-and-error era but, overall, faith in the project has been justified and Shuaiba will surely expand. Capital cost of the area up to March 1972, was KD. 15,719,209 (about $48 million) and operational and other services cost KD. 4,254,596 (about $14 million). The Authority's products brought in KD. 5,061,562 (about $17 million).

The first industry to start production in the area was the Kuwait Chemical Fertiliser Company in which the Kuwait Petrochemical Industries Company held 60 per cent of the capital, British Petroleum 20 per cent and the Gulf Research and Development Company 20 per cent. In 1973, the Petrochemical

Overleaf: Some Kuwait oil contains large amounts of sulphur, which is extracted at refineries near the Saudi Arabian border

Diversification

Industries Company took over sole ownership. The plant started production of sulphuric acid and liquid ammonia and ammonium sulphate in 1966. Production of urea fertiliser started in 1967. Progress has been steady, rising from a total production of 69,798 metric tons in 1966 to 423,807 metric tons in 1972. The major part of the production is exported to the countries of Southeast Asia, East Africa and the neighbouring Arab countries through Shuaiba harbour. The remainder is exported overland.

The Petrochemical Industries Plant situated on the coastline is owned by a Kuwaiti joint stock company and consists of two units for the manufacture of liquid ammonia, each unit having a capacity of 680 tons a day, and two units producing 700 tons of urea a day. This is one of the largest fertiliser plants in the world. In 1972, 586,332 metric tons of products were exported by the Kuwait Chemical Fertiliser Company and the Petrochemical Industries Company through the harbour—a striking contrast with the 1966 total of 9,343 metric tons. By land both companies exported 17,578 metric tons in 1972 (2,359 metric tons in 1966). In 1972 both companies employed 1,064 workers in various categories of which 55 were Kuwaitis. Since then there has been an increase in the number of Kuwaitis undergoing training for skilled employment—238 at the last count.

Shuaiba accommodates the world's first all-hydrogen operated refinery which is owned by the Kuwait National Petroleum Company. There are 15 productive units: the Burgan gas unit, hydrogen unit, sulphur unit, catalytic reformer unit, crude and vacuum unit, H. oil reactor unit, Isomax unit, naphtha unifiner unit, naphtha factionation unit, kerosene unifiner unit, light diesel unifiner unit, heavy diesel unifiner unit, amine unit treatment, ammoniacal water treatment unit, and nitrogen unit. The refinery possesses two of the biggest units in the world for hydrogen production and an outstanding component of the plant is the H. oil reactor which de-sulphurises and changes heavy oil residue into light products. The sulphur producing unit has a capacity of 205,000 tons annually. Products of the refinery, which have reached 135,000 barrels a day, are of very high quality and purity, particularly the sulphur residues. In 1972, total exports were 5,361,847 metric tons—5,221,643 metric tons through the oil pier and 140,294 metric tons by land. Of a staff of 648 at the end of 1972 a total of 81 Kuwaitis held key positions.

The oil industry is also served by the Dresser (Kuwait) Company plant which produces two main types of drilling mud, barite and bentonite, used

Right: A tank storage farm, located near the sea loading terminals

96

Above and right: The
Kuwait Flour Mills plant
in the Shuwaikh area;
flour milling is one of the
major local industries

in drilling oil wells. In 1972 the plant produced 14,141 tons. The Kuwait Industrial Refinery Maintenance and Engineering Company plant, which cost KD. 180,000,000 (about US $610 million) performs necessary services for heavy industries and manufactures boilers and heat exchangers. In 1971, the total value of services amounted to KD. 418,062 (US $1.42 million).

The Kuwait Cement Company, established by an Amiri Decree in 1968 with a capital of KD. 2.5 million (US $7.5 million), has an annual capacity of 300,000 tons of bagged and bulk Portland, ordinary and sulphate resistant cement. Clinker and gypsum are imported from the neighbouring Iraq under an agreement reached in 1970 with the Iraqi General Exportation Company. The output is marketed locally. A planned second stage of development depends on the results of geological surveys for raw materials in Kuwait. A total production of 700,000 tons a day is foreseen. In 1972, 61,817 tons of ordinary cement, 17,715 tons of middle resistance cement and 5,149 tons of sulphate resistant cement were produced.

The Kuwait United Fisheries Company, formed by an amalgamation of three Kuwaiti fishing companies, has its plants at the barge harbour which accommodates the fishing fleet and feeds in shrimps and other kinds of fish for processing. The various departments include a mechanical workshop, refrigeration rooms with a capacity of 1,200 tons, production sections equipped for processing and freezing shrimps with production running at 40 tons a day, the fish-meal plant for animal food with a daily production of 10 tons and the cod-liver oil by-product division.

The Nitrogen, Oxygen and Argon Plant which is owned by the Kuwait Oxygen and Acetylene Company produces industrial and medical gases to meet the nitrogen, oxygen and argon requirements of petroleum and petro-chemical industries. Production capacity is: 200 cubic metres/hour of liquid nitrogen, 200 cubic metres/hour of liquid oxygen and 4.5 cubic metres/hour of argon. The plant has a high storage capacity and is connected with neighbouring main consumers by a pipeline network. The final cost of the plant was more than KD.500,000 (US$1.7 million). In addition to its nitrogen, oxygen and argon production the plant manufactures ammonia for local consumption and for export to Middle East countries.

The Kuwait Sulphur Plant, on which work started at the end of 1972, grinds raw sulphur produced by the Kuwait National Petroleum Company and the American Independent Oil Company (Aminoil) for export through Shuaiba harbour. Annual production is about 15,000 metric tons. The

Oxygen, Nitrogen and Argon Plant of the Refrigeration and Oxygen Factory Company (Kuwait) produces oxygen, nitrogen and argon mainly for local use. Annual capacity is: oxygen 240,000 cubic metres, nitrogen 216,000 cubic metres and argon 10,800 cubic metres. Future plans for the area include the setting up of a polythene and polypropylene bags plant, an expansion of the KNPC refinery, petrochemical and gas utilisation project, a lubricating oil factory and extension to the Kuwait Cement Company's plant.

Not so long ago Kuwait imported practically all of its industrial requirements. The picture has been altered and today there is a steady stream of exports from Shuaiba which has effectively changed the one-industry image of Kuwait. Another large industrial complex is located at Shuwaikh, again in close proximity to the power-and-water distillation plants. The industries there are part of the ever-expanding Kuwait industrial scene which now supports no less than 450 different enterprises from metal-pipe factories to macaroni mills.

Next to oil itself, probably the most important single commodity in an oil-producing State is steel pipes and Kuwait has gone a long way to reduce its dependence on imports of this vital product. The Kuwait Metal Pipe Industries was set up by an Amiri Decree in 1966 and two years later spiral welded pipes began to roll off the production line. By 1969, production had reached 93,000 tons a year and this steadily increased as new machinery was added. In 1974, the industry produced 33,749 tons of pipes ranging from 10.75 inches to 48 inches in diameter. Exports play a large part in the factory's annual output and, in 1974, 19,500 tons were exported to Saudi Arabia, 260 tons to Iraq, 230 tons to Bahrain and 13,750 tons to Syria. A new plant is being established on a site of some 150,000 square metres and when this is in operation the company will have six production lines instead of three. There will be new equipment to turn out varieties of pipes in many sizes. The annual output will then reach 70,000 tons. The labour force in 1974 was 273 and an ambitious training programme has been undertaken to ensure an adequate supply of skilled workers.

Another important industry, linked with the government's low-income housing programme, is the Kuwait Prefabricated Building Company, established in 1964 by the Kuwait Industries Company and the Kuwait Investment Company with a capital of KD. 500,000 (about $1.7 million). Two years later, the Savings and Credit Bank joined in the venture as third and equal partner and the capital was raised to KD. 750,000 (about $2,500,000). In 1967, after

Below: Part of the Sea Island complex, where supertankers load

building villas by conventional methods, the company began manufacturing prefabricated elements and by the end of the year 176 two-storey, low-income group houses had been completed. The production rate was one house every two days. Later, this was increased to three houses a day—each comprising a surface area of 159 square metres in two storeys and consisting of 56 elements.

In 1969, the first three-storey prefabricated building (1,800 square metres) was built in Kuwait. In 1970, a large school and more than 300 houses were completed. In 1972, nine schools were built and the production of low-income houses at three every day proceeded. In 1974, the company completed two large government buildings: a four-storey Customs structure and a central store for the Ministry of Posts, Telegraphs and Telephones. In addition, vast quantities of culverts and other pre-cast structures have gone into Kuwait's seashore projects. These are providing the State with many miles of ultra-modern promenade, marina, sea clubs and other recreational facilities. By the end of 1975, a pre-stressed hollow-core concrete plant was due to go into operation and ten-storey, high-rise buildings were on the drawing boards.

Other successful enterprises in the Shuwaikh district include the Kuwait Flour Mills Company, which produces bread and many other flour products, a car-battery factory, a brickworks and many other subsidiary plants.

Government policy on industrialisation has developed in two fields: those industries which have a good domestic market and those which depend on petroleum as their raw material. Thus the Kuwait National Industries Company produces sand-lime bricks, asbestos pipes and sheets and cement bricks to supply the country with all its needs of these products. Kuwait's geographical position has always provided excellent opportunities to trade with the outside world. The ancient fleets and caravans used to stop in Kuwait on their way to the East and Kuwaitis, therefore, have had long experience in business and commercial matters. The country has always had a liberal commercial policy and, today, its programme of diversification of industries reflects the astute thinking of a people who have always occupied a prominent regional place in skilled craftsmanship.

Indicative of the success of government are the annual profits announced by the various enterprises established under the diversification programme. The Petrochemical Industries Company (PIC) for instance, in 1973 realised a profit of KD. 3.7 million (about $12.5 million). The ammonia and urea production units (which are separate from those of the Kuwait Chemical

Fertiliser Company, its subsidiary) operated at 76.2 per cent and 101.7 per cent of capacity respectively during the year. In 1972 the company produced 290,526 metric tons of liquid ammonia. In 1973, the output rose to 377,080 metric tons. Urea production also showed a rise. In 1972, the company produced 357,641 metric tons and this was increased to 399,000 metric tons in 1973. A total of 401,659 tons of urea was marketed in the year and the profits realised enabled the company to cover the accumulated losses of the previous year.

The subsidiary Kuwait Chemical Fertiliser Company, wholly owned by PIC, produced 105,000 tons of liquid ammonia in 1973. Other totals were: 181,000 tons of urea, 119,000 tons of ammonium sulphate and 103,000 tons of sulphuric acid. From its small beginning to the end of 1974 PIC has produced for world markets 1,889,950 metric tons of ammonia, 658,821 metric tons of ammonium sulphate and 2,112,056 metric tons of urea. At the end of 1974, the company's three ammonia plants had a total capacity of 700,000 metric tons a year, its three urea plants 644,000 metric tons, its ammonium sulphate plant an annual capacity of 165,000 metric tons and the sulphuric acid plant 132,000 metric tons. The company also owned and operated a salt and chlorine plant, producing salt, caustic soda, hydrochloric acid, hydrogen, chlorine and sodium hypochlorite. In the future it plans to move into new areas of chemical industries which will use the gas from oilfields in an ambitious programme for the manufacture of olefins, aromatics and other products.

Industrial diversification posed problems. For Kuwait the venture was new and there was no basis of experience, as in the older industrialised countries, to rely on. Nevertheless, the planning had been wise in the selection of enterprises that could rely on natural sources of fuel and on local markets for products. There were the initial losses of fledgling industries but, in time, these were overcome as Kuwait itself developed and avenues of sales broadened considerably. In addition, export markets were found in the Gulf region where the bounty of oil provided the money for similar development programmes. Today, though small by comparison with the industrial empires of the western nations and Japan, Kuwait's selected enterprises have proved their economic value and though oil must remain the predominant earner of revenue there is no doubt that diversification has provided a regular source of income for the large work-force that has been absorbed and profits for the companies involved.

Shipping

The debate over the pattern that diversification of industry in Kuwait should take is a continuing one but there never have been any doubts about the development of shipping activities which pre-date oil and which have traditionally established the fame of the State as the home of seafarers and of the craftsmen who built the sturdy vessels in which they carried on a lucrative mercantile business with India, East Africa and regions beyond.

The advent of oil has changed the structure of Kuwait's maritime activities. No longer are the dhows the mainstay of the State's shipping activities. They remain, of course, but in smaller number and their presence in the small dhow basins of Kuwait Bay is overshadowed by the leviathans which, in ever-increasing number, congregate in the harbour awaiting berths in the massive and modern expanse of Kuwait's Shuwaikh port.

The flags of all the maritime nations may be seen in Kuwait today—a tribute to the phenomenal rise of the State to international prominence since the first flow of oil made the progressive transformation from regional obscurity to modern nationhood possible. The Kuwaiti flag—as it did in the old dhow days—signifies Kuwait's emergence as a maritime power, today as in the past the biggest operator of a merchant marine in the Arab world.

In the past two decades the private sector in Kuwait has invested a large amount of capital in shipping and it was the business community that made the first initiative with the formation in 1957 of the Kuwait Oil Tanker Company (KOTC). The initial capital was KD5,751,345 (one Kuwaiti Dinar today equals about $3.50) and this was doubled in 1968. In 1959, the first tanker, Kazimah, was built by Sasebo Heavy Industries in Japan—at that time at 49,000 tons one of the world's big ships.

After that, two identical ships, Warbah and Al Sabbiyah, each of 60,000 tons, were built by Sasebo and in 1969 the same firm constructed the first VLCC (very large crude carrier), Arabiyeh of 208,000 tons.

In 1970, two VLCCs, Al Funtas and Al Badiah, each of 208,000 tons were added to the fleet and four years later a mammoth ULCC (ultra large crude carrier) of 361,000 tons, Al Andalus, was ordered from the Astano Shipyard in Spain to give the KOTC at present a fleet totalling 1,154,000 dwt.

More ships, however, are on order. By the end of 1976 three more vessels will join the fleet: two ULCCs of 400,000 tons each being built by Mitsubishi Heavy Industries in Japan and another of 328,000 tons now on the stocks at Chantier de la Ciotat in France.

By June, 1977, a 261,000-ton tanker, built by Sasebo Heavy Industries, is due to go into service. Thus, by 1977 the KOTC will be operating a fleet of more than 2,000,000 dwt—a total of 11 ships.

The KOTC, which distributed its first dividend in 1960, is the oldest company of its kind in the Arab world. In a recent interview, KOTC chairman, Mr. Abul Aziz Al Sager, proudly pointed to the fact that in 1975 KOTC tonnage was near or equal that of the whole Arab world combined.

The company is in the happy position of being able to look with equanimity at the slump in the international tanker market since preference—as in the past—will be given to its vessels for the carrying of Kuwaiti crude. From the beginning, KOTC's full tanker capacity was under charter to British Petroleum and Gulf Oil (former co-owners of the Kuwait Oil Company), most of it employed on the European run. Sales contracts with other purchasers now include the same condition so that the scope for expansion of business is big. Formerly, a relatively small proportion of Kuwaiti oil was carried under the Kuwaiti flag.

As Mr. Omar Taher Al Zeil, the company's general manager, told the author in April, 1976, "Most of our tankers used to be chartered to BP and Gulf. Of course, we are all affected by the slump in tanker business but we have some privileges in bunkering our ships. We get bunkers at a cheap price—about $25 a ton instead of the usual price of about $75 a ton. Bunkering plays a big role in operating expenses when you think that prevailing freight rates do not even reach break-even level and 45 million tons of shipping are laid up."

He said that, at present, KOTC tankers cannot carry more than ten per cent of Kuwaiti production but that other Arab-owned vessels, such as those of the Arab Maritime Petroleum Transport Company (AMPTC), founded by the Organisation of Arab Petroleum Exporting Countries (OAPEC), could be used.

KOTC's cumulative net profit during the 1960–73 period amounted to KD17.1 million and dividends paid to KD12.3 million over that period. Total income in 1974 amounted to KD11,208,272, an increase of 31.50 per cent over that of 1973 (KD8,526,553). Expenses, including depreciation, amounted to

Above: A dhow basin in Kuwait City

104

KD6,437,658 as against KD6,326,562 in 1973, an increase of 1.7 per cent. Thus net profits in 1974 amounted to KD4,770,614 against KD2,199,991 in 1973, an increase of about 117 per cent. This made a cumulative net profit from 1960 to 1974 of approximately KD21.85 million.

With a large building programme in hand and with expansion plans in mind, particularly concerning the transportation of refined products and LPG, the company decided in 1974 to increase its capital from KD11,502,690 to KD13,228,095 by issing 230,054 shares at a nominal value of KD7.500.

In a review of Kuwait's shipping activities in February, 1975, *The Times* said, "Virtually the only countries active in the new ship-contracting market have been the Arab nations and, most notably, Saudi Arabia and Kuwait, both of which are setting the pace in building up their own domestic fleets through their own shipping companies and through others in which Arab nations are participants.

"In recent months it has been Kuwait that has emerged as an increasingly important force, although this is hardly surprising considering the nation's traditional links with the sea. For generations, before the exploitation of the region's oil reserves began on a large scale, Kuwaitis were sailing their dhows on the trade routes between the Gulf and India and East Africa—and even farther south and east in search of trade. The development of Kuwait's oil reserves resulted in diminished maritime activity but now buttressed by the tremendous inflow of oil revenue after the events of 1973–74 (when prices were raised) the development of a modern and efficient merchant fleet, embracing dry cargo and tanker tonnage, is being accorded a priority status."

The KOTC London office took over the management of the fleet at the end of 1973 and there are about 25 people there, mostly technical personnel. This move has greatly facilitated tanker maintenance and has overcome the problem of undue stoppage of tankers which was a source of great concern in the past.

Other than the tanker business the KOTC runs an agency branch which services all tankers calling at the loading terminals at Mena Al Ahmadi, Mena Abdulla, Ras Khafji and Kuwait itself. In a year the agency handles more than 2,000 tankers. Services include the repair of radar, radio and electronic equipment aboard the ships.

The KOTC is, also, through its gas branch, the exclusive distributor of LPG for domestic use in Kuwait. The LPG filling plant is fully automatic

105

Left: The Al-Ahmadi port for oil loading. Below: The Kuwait Oil Company's North Pier, which is for smaller tankers

Shipping with the capability of producing more than 15,000 cylinders of 12 kilograms daily. KOTC lorries carry the cylinders to all areas of Kuwait for use in most kitchens. In 1974, for instance, no less than 2,545,334 cylinders of LPG were distributed.

In the dry cargo field the past decade has seen a steady expansion of the Kuwait Shipping Company, originally established in May, 1965, with the State taking an initial 60 per cent shareholding in the concern. Founding capital was KD2 million. The origins of the company, however, go back to 1962 when a group of merchants and shipping agents set up a committee to consider forming a fleet. By the time the plant had been formulated in 1965, the private sector was reluctant to go ahead alone because of the depressed business climate then, but Shaikh Jabir Al Ahmed Al Sabah, the present Heir Apparent and Prime Minister, decided that the long-term prospects were good and that the State should take the initiative. Since then the Government has never interfered in the internal affairs of the company which has always operated on a purely commercial basis.

The company started business in 1965 with second-hand and chartered ships but almost immediately placed an order worth $40 million for 16 vessels, 13 of 13,440 dwt and three of 16,000 dwt which were delivered in the 1967–72 period when the capital was increased to KD9 million and the company received substantial loans from the State. In the light of considerable congestion being suffered in other Gulf ports, together with the rise in dues and demurrage charges, KSC then decided to embark on a big expansion.

There followed orders, amounting to £75 million, for nine 22,300 tons vessels from the Upper Clyde Yard (now Govan Shipbuilders) in Scotland. In 1973, the company also purchased two smaller 9,100 dwt vessels from Spain to operate in the Gulf and Red Sea area. Then in 1974 orders were placed for 15 ships described as "carbon copies" of the Govan ones from Hyundai Shipbuilding and Heavy Industries of South Korea as well as another three from Spain. By August, 1977, the company's fleet will consist of 47 vessels of an overall deadweight of 1,000,000 tons.

There will be 30 sailings a year to the United Kingdom, northern Europe and Iran, 24 sailings to the Far East and 18 to the USA. By 1980, the sailings will be increased by the addition of more vessels which will bring the fleet total to about 100 ships.

But long before that—in July, 1975—the name, Kuwait Shipping Company, disappeared and was replaced by that of the United Arab Shipping Company,

Above: Kuwait Oil Tanker Company's first tanker, 1959, the *Kazimah*

formed following an agreement with the Gulf states of Saudi Arabia, Iraq, Bahrain, Oman, the United Arab Emirates and Qatar to establish a joint shipping enterprise with a capital of KD500 million.

At the time of formation, the other Gulf states had not offered any ships but provision was made for companies in the private sector to participate through their governments if they wished to join the new company.

The KSC employs mainly British officers but an extensive programme is under way to train Kuwaiti cadets who, it is hoped, will eventually operate the fleet. Seamen are mainly from Pakistan and Sierra Leone.

Increasing the KSC's profits are its subsidiaries The Kuwait Shipping agency has a branch in Dubai as well as representative offices elsewhere. It has a share in Aratrans Kuwait, a forwarding company, in partnership with Kuwait Airways. It also owns Kuwait Chartering on a 50–50 basis with Wallace Shipping. The company has also participated in the capital of the Kuwait Supply Company and the Kuwait International Exhibitions Company.

The technical branch of the company is located in the British north-western port of Liverpool where 85 people are employed. All the technical services such as the ordering of spare parts and dry-docking programmes are arranged there.

Capital of the company at the beginning of 1976 was KD21 million. In 1974, the profit was by far the largest in the company's history at KD6,127,743 compared with KD2,028,163 in 1973. The improvement followed expansion of

Shipping the fleet units, of the company's activities worldwide and of subsidiaries.

There is no doubt that with regular services operating to European ports, the United Kingdom, Japan and the United States and with the development of further routes and an expansion of present sailing schedules the KSC—or, in its new form, the United Arab Shipping Company—will play a major role in the development of the Gulf area and Kuwait.

Apart from its own crude oil and products carrier operations, Kuwait is one of the ten partners in the Arab Maritime Petroleum Transport Company (AMPTC) formed through the Organization of Arab Petroleum Exporting Countries (OAPEC) which has its headquarters in Kuwait.

According to projections by AMPTC, the aggregate tanker fleet of the Arab national oil transport companies that are AMPTC members is scheduled to rise from 32 units of 3,131,787 dwt in December, 1975, to 55 units with a capacity of 7,877,787 dwt by April, 1978.

At present, the Arab tanker fleet is relatively modern and by 1978 will be among the biggest in the world. Combining current tonnage with future deliveries AMPTC figures show that by 1978 this joint company itself should have the largest tanker fleet (2,371,665 dwt) followed by Kuwait (2,137,000 dwt), Iraq (1,279,000 dwt), Libya (1,176,500 dwt), Abu Dhabi (530,132 dwt), Algeria (275,900 dwt) and Saudi Arabia (107,590 dwt).

Further activity can be expected from the AMPTC and from the indigenous Kuwait shipping companies in the next few years in line with their policy of ensuring that a substantial volume of their country's trade, whether in oil or cargoes, should be carried in nationally operated tonnage. Kuwait has set the pace in the development of a modern and efficient fleet and clearly intends to remain in the forefront.

On a smaller scale Kuwaitis are engaged in other shipping activities. For some years, various individual Kuwaitis have owned their own private vessels, primarily for transporting livestock from Australia. In 1974, they joined forces and amalgamated their maritime assets by forming the Kuwait Livestock Transport Company.

The Kuwait Investment Company has two shipping enterprises. One operates four cargo vessels of about 12,000 dwt including two equipped with refrigeration for the transport of vegetables and fruits between the Mediterranean and the UK. The second one operates a "roll-on/roll-off" car ferry service between the UK and Ireland with two other vessels. Another two were ordered last year and are due to come into service in 1977.

Fishing has long been a major industry in Kuwait and the tradition has been maintained by the establishment of the United Fisheries of Kuwait, an amalgamation of the Gulf Fisheries, the National Fisheries and the International Fisheries, with a capital fund of about $30 million and more than $60 million assets.

The company in 1975 operated a fleet of more than 150 vessels, including factory boats, working over a vast area which included the Red Sea, off Muscat, North and South Yemen, Nigeria, Mauretania, Senegal, Madagascar and New Guinea. Today the company is one of the biggest shrimp producers in the world and its lobster operations have rapidly extended to make it a serious competitor to the major fishing nations.

All agreements between the company and the countries off which its fleet operates are based on the principle of equal participation associated usually with national development plans so as to bring maximum economic benefit to the participants. In many cases the company provides short-term loans where capital is not available. The objectives are to develop the fishing industries of the countries in agreement with the United Fisheries and to assist developing countries to profit from their own sea-wealth. Thus, crews are taken on locally in whichever country's waters the ships are operating.

The company is extending year by year. New vessels are constantly on order—stern trawlers of 500-ton capacity and side trawlers of equal capacity for lobster, mid- and deep-sea fishing. There are slipways in Kuwait and off the island of Napa, near Australia, and in Nigeria.

The shrimp and fish-processing plant at Shuaiba in Kuwait is one of the most modern in the world. It handles 100 tons of produce daily and includes a fishmeal plant where shrimp waste and trash fish are ground along with other fish to make animal foodstuffs.

Onshore and offshore the company in 1975 employed more than 3,000 personnel who were widely international in their origins. The main exports are to Japan, the United States and Europe but other regions, including the Middle East, are served.

Over-fishing and pollution in the Gulf have resulted in smaller shrimp catches and the company believes that a collective effort by the riparian states in the Gulf is necessary to tackle the problems of pollution and over-fishing. Last year, the UN Food and Agricultural Organization undertook a research programme in the Gulf and it is hoped that this may lead to a cooperative effort to improve the prospects of the fishing industry.

Above and left: Part of the extensive port facilities at Ahmadi; the oil flows by gravity down a gentle slope to the loading terminals

Kuwait's port facilities are modern and extensive. Oil is the major export and the Kuwait Oil Company possesses two shore loading terminals, the South Pier, commissioned in 1949, and the North Pier, which commenced operations in 1959. The South Pier is able to berth up to eight ships, including some of 100,000 tons capacity. The North Pier can accommodate four ships of up to 200,000 tons capacity.

Increases in annual production and the appearance of super-tankers made it necessary to supplement the shore loading terminals, and the Sea Island terminal was constructed about ten miles from the coast. This was commissioned in 1969. It is able to berth two ships of up to 500,000 tons capacity each. On a smaller scale, the other oil companies in Kuwait have their own loading terminals.

In the early part of 1952, the Kuwait Development Board was set up by the Government and among its projects was the designing of the port at Shuwaikh. It was completed in July, 1960, and is one of the greatest projects carried out in the country.

The new port has four berths for 600-feet vessels or ships with a depth of 33 feet, three more berths for medium-sized ships of not more than 18 feet draught, two berths on buoys, a harbour for small craft, launches, fishing boats and barges, another for yachts and another for Government boats, salvage barges, pilot cutters and tugs.

The jetties were equipped with electric cranes, mobile cranes, large storage sheds and many other modern facilities which have been augmented by new equipment. Kuwait also possesses small dock basins capable of receiving dhows which are still engaged in extensive coastal trading.

While the port at Shuwaikh revolutionised the country's maritime activities, it soon became apparent that extensions would be needed to cope with increased trade by sea. Deep berths were increased to nine. Three berths were built with facilities for unloading cattle and other livestock and a quarantine building was erected. A basin for fishing craft followed the cold-storage buildings and provision was made for a jetty for dhows when the tremendous scheme for turning Kuwait's entire coastline into a leisure esplanade comes into effect.

With the creation of the vast Shuaiba Industrial Area in Kuwait it became apparent that port facilities would be needed there for both oil-product export and commercial imports and exports. The main purpose in providing port facilities was to serve existing establishments as well as future enter-

Right: One of the Kuwait
Oil Tanker Company's
latest tankers, a VLCC
(Very Large Crude-oil
Carrier), the *Al Badiah*

prises. Construction of the harbour began in 1964 and was completed in 1967. The harbour's main facilities comprise three parts:

The Commercial Harbour. The handling capacity of this section is about one million tons. Its jetty is 650 metres in length with a width of 100 metres. It accommodates warehouses, the harbour master's building, cranes and other equipment. There are five berths varying in depth from 23 to 27 feet.

The Barge Harbour. This is completely protected and provides berths for tugs and other service boats belonging to the Authority as well as other smaller craft. It also accommodates fishing trawlers and the United Fisheries plant is located on one of the quays.

Oil Pier. The oil pier extends from the end of the harbour approach to 1,000 metres into the sea with a width of 16 metres. Four metres of its width serve as a road while the remaining eight metres support the pipe network which carries the liquid products of the Kuwait National Petroleum Company refinery as well as the liquid ammonia of the Petrochemical Industries Company, both situated in Shuaiba.

The pier has two 45-feet-depth berths. The outer one, which extends 320 metres, can accommodate tankers of up to 100,000 tons deadweight. The inner one, about 300 metres, accommodates tankers up to 40,000 dwt.

Within a short time after the construction of the harbour, plans were on the drawing boards for an expansion of facilities to cope with increased demand. The first project was for the expansion in stages of the commercial harbour by six berths, each 200 metres in length and about 13 metres deep with provision for deepening to 14 metres. There was also a threefold project to extend the oil pier and to improve the engineering services. Two berths, one to accommodate tankers of 40,000 dwt and the other to handle 100,000 dwt tankers, were added early in 1975.

Early in 1975, the Kuwait Shipbuilding and Repairyard Company signed contracts for the construction of shipbuilding and repair facilities in Kuwait, including a dry dock, as part of the extension of Shuwaikh port. The project was due for completion in five years.

Thus, Kuwait with its abundance of capital may be expected to become steadily stronger in world shipping. As a service sector, it has the attraction of not requiring the import of foreign labour. Shipping fits in well with the deeply engrained mercantile mentality of the State. It is not without good reason that the symbol of Kuwait is a dhow, rather than a drilling rig or a petrol pump.

AL BADIAH

البادية

Below: A part of the
University of Kuwait.
Upper right: The futuristic
Kuwait Towers will serve
a double purpose, providing
water and recreational
facilities. Above and below
right: Houses for people of
limited income

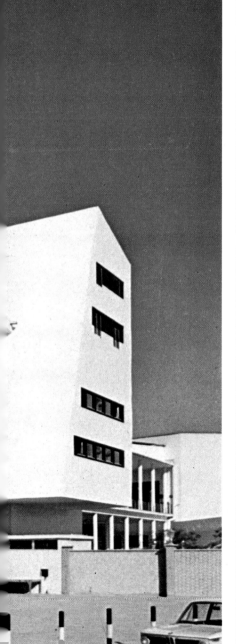

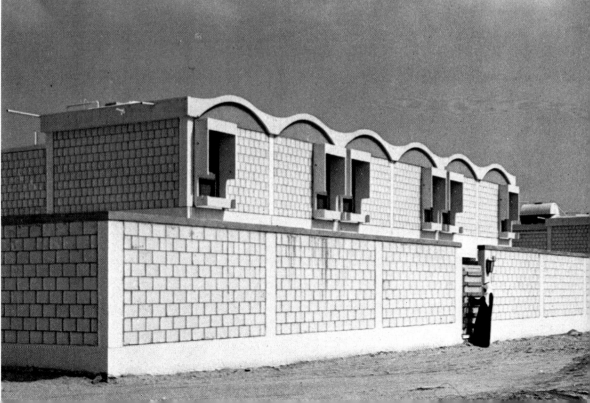

Riding High

Road communications in Kuwait are now among the best in the world and a pattern of wide, high-speed highways links Kuwait City with the main oilfield regions, including Ahmadi, headquarters of the Kuwait Oil Company. In addition, the limitless flat expanse of the desert has been traversed by motorways, brilliantly lit, which connect the State with Iraq and Saudi Arabia. The stupendous growth of motor traffic has brought to Kuwait City itself the problem of the rush-hour crawl but, gradually, this is being eased by the construction of a dual-carriageway road crossing reclaimed land along the seafront of Kuwait Bay to the residential suburbs. When this has been landscaped it will become a scenic asset as well as a siphon to divert much of the heavy flow of traffic entering or leaving the metropolis from such suburbs as Salmieh or the oilfield regions.

Left: A view of the City fronting Kuwait Bay. Overleaf: The Kuwait Sheraton, built close to the boundary where the old town wall once stood

Roundabouts, which played a satisfactory role up to recent years in regulating the flow of traffic, are now being phased out everywhere and replaced by traffic lights. With many roads converging on a single roundabout it soon became evident that, with the heavy flow of traffic, the limitations of the system had become an accident hazard. In addition to the series of traffic lights the planners foresee in the near future the construction of fly-overs and subways to ease the chronic congestion of the present.

So far, apart from zebra crossings, which have not in any way lessened the hazards of crossing a road, no steps have been taken to protect the pedestrian outside the city area where traffic lights enable walkers to negotiate car-filled highways. The press has been specific in pinpointing the need for crossing points, such as bridges or under-passes, to be built in suburban areas and adjacent to the wide motorways which pass several built-up areas up to the Iraq and Saudi Arabian borders. The present priority, of course, is to continue road-building in a bid to reduce the flow of traffic on the main roads. Pedestrian crossing points will follow, particularly on such roads as the high-speed coastal motorway, so as to enable pedestrians to reach the beach along which a varied series of attractions are being built.

In 1964, a well-known town planner wrote: "One goes around in circles in Kuwait. And one travels around in Kuwait in a car. Walking here has in

ten short years become a lost and dead art. Distances in Kuwait in regard to the population are vast. The city extends over twenty kilometres from developed end to end. Therefore, distances are immense. This makes man in Kuwait totally dependent on a car." At that time Kuwait possessed no less than about 150 traffic roundabouts with more under construction. With remarkable foresight the expert predicted that the roundabout, like the dhow, was doomed to extinction as it became clear—as inevitably it would —that "the turnaround, rotary, roundabout of 'traffic circle', so used when the car was a novelty", was able only to cope with 10-mile-per-hour buggies.

Earlier, in 1960, another architectural expert wrote, "No doubt Kuwait has the best streets—really super-highways—of any city in the Arab world if not in the world at large." Fifteen years later, that statement still reflects the standing of Kuwait so far as the excellence of road communications is concerned. There are few countries which have spent so much money on road-making and there are few countries today that are tackling the traffic-congestion problem with such alacrity as Kuwait where, early in 1975, vast stretches of roads in the city itself and far beyond—some no more than ten years old—were being entirely relaid in a major effort to cope with the omnipresent automobile.

In Kuwait the element of speed—of doing things at the maximum pace— has characterised and dominated the build-up from township to capital city. Thus, in 1961, yet another urban planner had to look ahead to the 1970s and saw the day "when everyone in Kuwait owns a villa or two, four cars or five and has more than enough of all that the USA, Europe and Japan manufacture". By that time, he forecast, Kuwait would surely be one of the most "swankee" and up-to-date cities with first-class facilities of all sorts: port, airport, and highways; networks of housing, hospitals, schools and recreation areas; shopping areas, embassies and a government centre. By then Kuwait would have been perhaps the fastest built city in the world, providing for its inhabitants first-rate amenities and facilities of all types. And, by then, there probably would not be a single poor or neglected Kuwaiti. Indeed, by then, every Kuwaiti would be "very rich, well established in business and/or governmental position—in and out of Kuwait—with few pecuniary worries about housing, health, education pension and the future in general", he wrote.

The forecast was not wide of the mark. It would be rash to name every Kuwaiti as a millionaire in the two-villa or five-car league. The indigenous

121

Riding High   population, by and large, is economically dependent on wages or salaries and yet, compared with the situation in many other countries, the Kuwaiti lives in a modern Utopia in which social-welfare benefits generously distributed by the government have eased the burden of day-to-day existence.

One of the biggest road-building projects, the 95-kilometre Kuwait-Saudi Arabia highway, was completed in 1975. Like all the other road-building activities in the State it entailed the laying of sewage pipes, underground cables, water pipes and other installations involving several government ministries. This has been the pattern throughout—roads and their ancillary works: drainage outlets, sewers, telephone cables, water pipes, electricity cables, street-lighting circuits and so on. The Kuwait that has now taken shape is a very different place from the desert region with its compact coastal township that existed before the oil era. Modern Kuwait began in the early 1950s with an ambitious programme of tree-planting to break the desert winds and sandstorms, to try and stop erosion and irrigate what had been sandy wastelands. At breathtaking speed the new Kuwait took shape: houses, public buildings, office blocks, schools, hospitals, wide highways and shopping precincts.

The result has been the gift of attractive living to the population of the State but there is still a long way to go before Kuwait itself attains the architectural attractiveness that has been envisaged by the planners. So long as the basic work proceeds—the road-building, the laying of underground works and similar constructional activity—then the scenic additions must be held in abeyance. Outside of the main business area and some of the suburban shopping streets paved sidewalks are scarce in number. Hard-packed sand provides the base for the pedestrian. In times of high winds miniature dust-storms sweep through the suburbs and during the short period of rain the going underfoot becomes extremely muddy. Given completion of the main underground works, still proceeding apace everywhere, the laying of paved sidewalks will banish the hazards of walking and, on the sea front, the approach to the sandy foreshore will be scenically landscaped to transform the city into a riviera of the Middle East. The face of nearly six miles of waterfront will be dramatically changed with the dual carriageway from Shuwaikh along the shore to Dasman Point and the junction with the first ring road providing a modern backdrop for pleasure gardens, sea clubs, marinas, hotels and restaurants. When the ambitious programme has been finally completed it will represent a considerable tourist attraction though the main object is to beautify the coastline.

Much has been written about the architectural appearance of Kuwait. There are the critics, who argue that the planning was grandiose but not the composition, that though the buildings are excellent they offer an architectural hotch-potch of every regional style in the world. Yet in their bizarre conglomeration of ebullient styles the villas of the Kuwaitis present a rousing landscape of suburban non-conformity, altogether different from the regulated housing estates of Britain with their battalions of semi- or detached residences lined up in unchanging uniformity. Kuwait today offers one of the most unusual pieces of urbanisation in desert history. The drab, monotone face of the desert has been changed by sleek, sweeping super-highways alongside of which the strangest forms of buildings have taken shape. Where once there was hardly a tree to be seen today thousands of trees have been forced to grow.

Let the famous Arab architect and town-planner, Saba George Shiber, have the last word:

"Kuwait, the Pearl of the Gulf, is a fast evolving Arab metropolis. It is in a miraculous, meteoric race with time, having made perhaps the greatest jumps, leaps and strides within a decade-and-a-half of any other community anywhere in history. From a very elemental but tenacious type of sedentary existence, it has collapsed time into a small capsule, attaining great physical prowess and progress that stun the eyes and minds that have time to stop, see and think, to compare old with new, yesterday with today. The rate of change here is fast: perhaps the fastest—in relative terms—in history." These words were written in the early 1960s. In the 1970s they still hold true.

Skyways

The Kuwait Airways Corporation today ranks high among the world's international carriers with routes covering three continents and extending for several thousand miles. The Corporation in 1975 operated six Boeing 707-320Cs and its staff roll was around the 2,000 mark. Yet, just over 20 years ago, it was an infant company with no more than 20 staff members and two twin-engined Dakotas operating from a makeshift airport. Like the story of Kuwait itself the airline saga is one of iron-willed determination to match new affluence with the transition from regional obscurity to international standing. It is yet another success story from a State that has achieved staggering progress and, as an example of Kuwaiti enterprise, it reflects on an international scale the tremendous driving force that has activated Kuwait's great leap forward.

In 1953, a group of Kuwaiti businessmen decided to form an airline. They asked for government support, which was readily given, and in March 1954 the Kuwait National Airways Company Limited came into being. The new company bought two DC-3 aircraft, which were named *Warah* (after the first oil well discovered in Kuwait) and *Kazima* (an old district of Kuwait). The first regular scheduled service, to Basrah in Iraq, began in May 1954, but with the growing influx of people entering the country a third DC-3, *Al-Jahara*, was added to the fleet a year later and services were extended to Lebanon, Syria, Jordan, Saudi Arabia and Iran. A few months later the company's share capital was doubled with the acquisition by the government of a 50 per cent interest.

In those early days all engineering work was done in Beirut by the Middle East Aircraft Servicing Company, who stationed an engineer in Kuwait to handle the company's aircraft. Airport facilities were meagre, consisting of an open expanse of sand and Nissen huts. In the summer of 1956, two Hermes aircraft were purchased to cope with increased passenger traffic and new routes were started to Cairo, Bahrain and Dharan. A year later, two chartered DC-4s joined the service and the company's name was changed to Kuwait Airways Company. At the same time, Vickers Viscounts were introduced and new routes opened to India, Pakistan and all points on the Arabian Gulf.

The next four years saw a steady growth in the company's operations and it soon became apparent that an ambitious expansion plan would have to be undertaken to enable the airline to maintain its position as a major operator in the region. The shareholders decided that it was in the best interest of the enterprise for the State to assume full control and to provide the money required to finance the company's expansion. In 1962, the company's shareholders voted to sell all private shares to the State which then assumed full control and changed the operating name to that of the Kuwait Airways Corporation.

At that time, the first phase of the construction of the International Airport had been completed and the KAC transferred its operations there. On the assumption of government control the agreement with the British Overseas Airways Corporation, which had managed all operations, was terminated and the airline became completely independent. An expansion programme was immediately launched and a Comet 4-C was chartered. In 1963, another Comet was bought and a year later, after a decade of successful development, a third Comet joined the fleet. Older aircraft, like the Viscounts, were phased out and in March 1966, the Corporation introduced the Trident 1-E. In May of the same year it acquired a second Trident but, with the expansion of routes, it soon became evident that bigger jet aircraft would be needed and the Boeing 707-3200 was selected.

The first 707 went into service in January 1968, and two more were placed in service the same year. They enabled KAC to increase its weekly flights to Bombay from three to four and to London from four to five. Rome was also added to the network to enable the Corporation to maintain its share in the highly competitive air-transport market. With the introduction of the Boeings the Comets were immediately phased out and the Tridents were retained for a couple of years on short-range routes. The three original DC-3s were given to Jordan as a gift by the Amir. In 1971, the Tridents were finally withdrawn and two more Boeings were ordered. These joined the fleet early in 1972, making the airline an operator of a single make of aircraft. In 1963, Kuwait Airways was admitted to the International Air Transport Association as an active member. The airline also takes an active part in regional air-transport development and contributes towards the promotion and progress of commercial aviation in the Gulf area.

Today the KAC possesses an engineering complex of intricate sophistication and, with more than 500 engineers, mechanics and other technicians

operating in a hangar-workshop sprawl of huge buildings at the International Airport, it is the proud boast of the airline that a Boeing 707 can be completely stripped, repaired and re-assembled to conform with every international safety regulation. A recent survey conducted in Kuwait by an international air-transport publication concluded that the KAC fleet was "superbly equipped technically" with back-up facilities on hand to extend services to any part of the world. Such a situation would be praiseworthy anywhere with a long-established aviation tradition. In Kuwait, however, commercial aviation dates back scarcely more than a generation to 1948 when the Kuwait Oil Company began using aircraft to ferry company employees and bring in fresh fruit and vegetables.

The next development came several years later when the Kuwait Aero Club was formed, using small, single-engine, fabric-covered Austers to train

the first Kuwaiti pilots. At that time, engineers were recruited from Britain to service the planes and it was not until 1964 that the first Kuwaitis went to the United Kingdom to train as engineers and mechanics. Today, scores more have been trained at home and abroad and some of the first recruits now occupy key positions. Other technicians have been trained at the Boeing plant in Seattle, Washington, at Hawker-Siddeley and Rolls-Royce in Britain and at the Pratt and Whitney works in America.

The facilities at the maintenance base are staggering to the layman. The hangar is so large it can accommodate three Boeing 707s at one time and the support provided by the workshops is so extensive that an infinite number of functions can be carried out—from virtually taking apart and assembling an entire aircraft body to repairing giant jet engines, testing and assembling delicate flight instruments and re-upholstering passenger seats. Since it was

Skyways   inaugurated in the late 1960s KAC's Flight Training Centre has virtually eliminated the need to send any trainees overseas. Training is the key to air safety and all technical personnel in aviation in Kuwait, whether flight crew or workshop engineers, must hold ratings issued by the United Kingdom Civil Aviation Authority. The stage is now set for the Corporation to extend its eastern flights beyond Bombay, probably on to Tokyo, and in the West to reach the United States.

At a time when the international transport giants have been flying with empty seats and suffering huge revenue losses the KAC has established an enviable record, with annual turnover rising from KD. 3 million to KD. 14 million and a former loss of KD. 1.5 million now showing as a credit balance. The progress made by Kuwait Airways illustrates the new-found international status of this small country of less than one million people.

Health

The impressive progress made by Kuwait over the past twenty-five years is the direct result of the forward-thinking policy of a government which has used oil-wealth to provide incomparable social benefits for its population. Modern office blocks, schools, hospitals, parks and shopping centres now dominate the landscape and there is evidence everywhere of vast resources used not only to steer the country through an era of unparalleled growth but to provide a social-welfare system of remarkable official generosity, particularly in the fields of education and medicine.

Kuwait's health services are highly developed and in terms of range and quality they compare favourably with those of many advanced countries. The salient difference is that practically all facilities are extended free of charge. Hospitals are modern in design and medical personnel come from many countries to suit the skills and standards required. To supplement the work of the hospitals every suburb now has a modern clinic within easy reach of residents. All this has been accomplished at a rate rarely—if ever—achieved elsewhere. It reflects credit on an administration that, as soon as money became available in any volume, made certain that health and education programmes had the first calls on the budget. In 1949, there were only 4 doctors employed by the government. In 1973, the number of doctors in the health service had reached 800 with another 190 in private practice. There is 1 doctor in the country for every 1,078 persons. The total number of visits to public hospitals and dispensaries was 6,619,520 in 1973 and public current and capital expenditure on health services in 1973–74 was about KD. 25 million (about $85 million)—7.4 per cent of total government outlays.

In 1973, there were 11 hospitals and sanatoria, 42 clinics, 47 dental clinics, 11 mother and child centres, 12 preventive health centres and 270 school health clinics—all for a population less than one million in number. The exceptional range of skills offered is illustrated by 1973 statistics on fields of practice of physicians in the service: general practitioners, 410; cardiology, 7; nutritional specialist, 1; infectious diseases, 2; tropical diseases, 5; pediatrics, 55; pneumatology, 15; dermatology and venerology, 12; neurology and psychiatry, 9; anaesthesia, 14; general surgery, 27; orthopaedics, 14;

Previous pages: A Boeing 707 belonging to the Kuwait Airways Corporation. Overleaf: A special incubator unit at the Al-Sabah Hospital

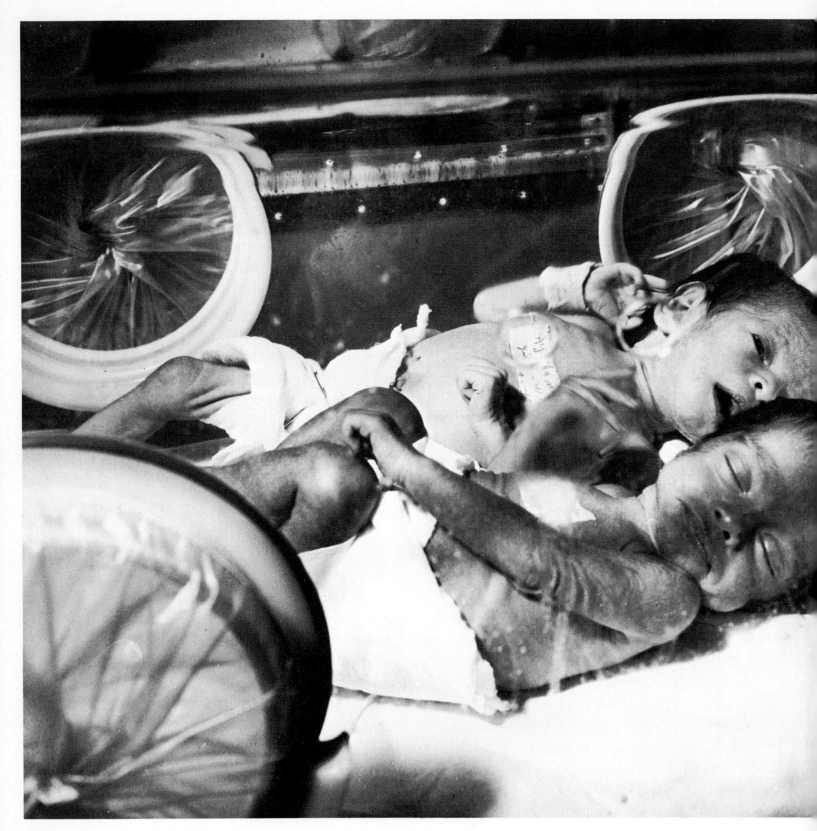

ophthalmology, 14; oto-rhino-laryncology, 12; analysis, 9; radiotherapy, 12; physical medicine, 4; preventive health, 5; occupational diseases, 5; dentists, 66; gynaecology, 60; others, 42. All these made a total of 800 physicians. The grand total of medical personnel in all fields employed in public hospitals and health centres in 1973 was 4,837. There were 3,731 beds with a total of 84,657 patients admitted to public hospitals. In the private sector there were 8 hospitals with a total of 400 beds and a total staff of about 1,000.

The Amiri Hospital, completed in 1949 and soon to be replaced by a completely new 500-bed hospital, was the first step in the social service programme. Soon mental hospitals, sanatoria, maternity units and a new general hospital were under construction. The most advanced diagnostic and therapeutic equipment was bought by Kuwait on an enormous scale and the Al Sabah Hospital, opened in 1962, marked the culmination of an era of intensive activity and heavy spending on welfare services. The Al Sabah Hospital, occupying 407,000 square feet, cost about $10 million. It has a helicopter pad to bring in patients from the island territories and the desert.

In 1952, Kuwait opened its first sanatorium for the treatment of tuberculosis. It contained 100 beds, but temporary accommodation for women patients had to be found later. In 1959, however, a massive sanatorium which was in every respect a model TB treatment centre was opened on the sea front in the Shuwaikh district of Kuwait City. It consisted of a three-storey, air-conditioned building with every conceivable facility for treatment and recuperation, including a recreational garden. As a result, the incidence of TB has been drastically reduced in the State.

Overall responsibility has been that of the Ministry of Public Health. Its growth has been commensurate with Kuwait's massive expansion and its many departments include those supervising administrative duties, technical developments, the legal and investigation side, preventive medicine, finance, all medical services and the pharmaceutical branches. Up to the discovery of oil and the formation of the Kuwait Oil Company with the social services it rapidly established there was only one small mission hospital, set up in 1911 at the request of the late Shaikh Mubarak Al Sabah, a wise and far-sighted ruler. Dr. C. S. G. Mylrea, an Englishman who worked for thirty years in Kuwait and is buried there, Dr. Arthur Bennett and Dr. Paul Harrison were members of the Arabian Mission of the Dutch Reformed Church of America which provided a much smaller population—about 60,000 in 1939—with a then much-needed medical service.

131

The Maternity Hospital,
one of the most modern
of Kuwait's Hospitals

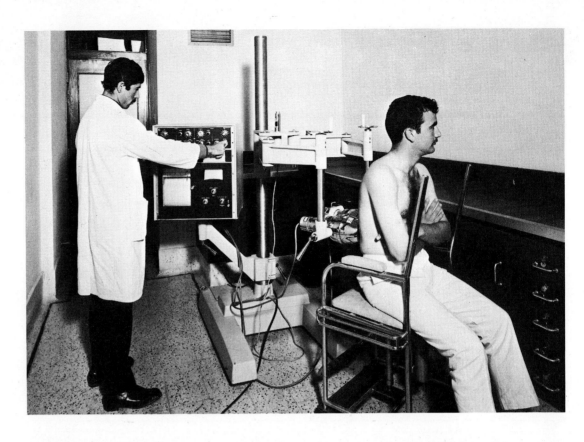

Above: Kuwait's hospitals provide modern facilities for all. Right: An operation in progress at the Al-Sabah Hospital

In 1932, Kuwait lived through its last great smallpox epidemic. More than 4,000 people died in about ten days. Today, a vast preventive service, which started with large-scale inoculation in 1952, has reduced the disease to insignificance, just as tuberculosis has been controlled. In few places has money been used so speedily and effectively to conquer disease and employ the most modern equipment available to protect the health of everyone in the State.

Indicative of Kuwait's importance as a country well advanced in medical technology and resources was its choice in 1974 as the venue for the twelfth conference of the Arab Medical Association. More than 350 physicians from the Arab world attended the conference and saw, in many cases with some envy, the multifarious medical services bestowed on the populace by an enlightened administration. One of the earliest hospitals established in Kuwait was the Kuwait Oil Company's Southwell Hospital in Ahmadi. Following Kuwait's assumption of total control of the oil company this well-equipped hospital was made available for use by the general public. Formerly all patients had been company personnel and members of their families. The name has been changed to Ahmadi Hospital.

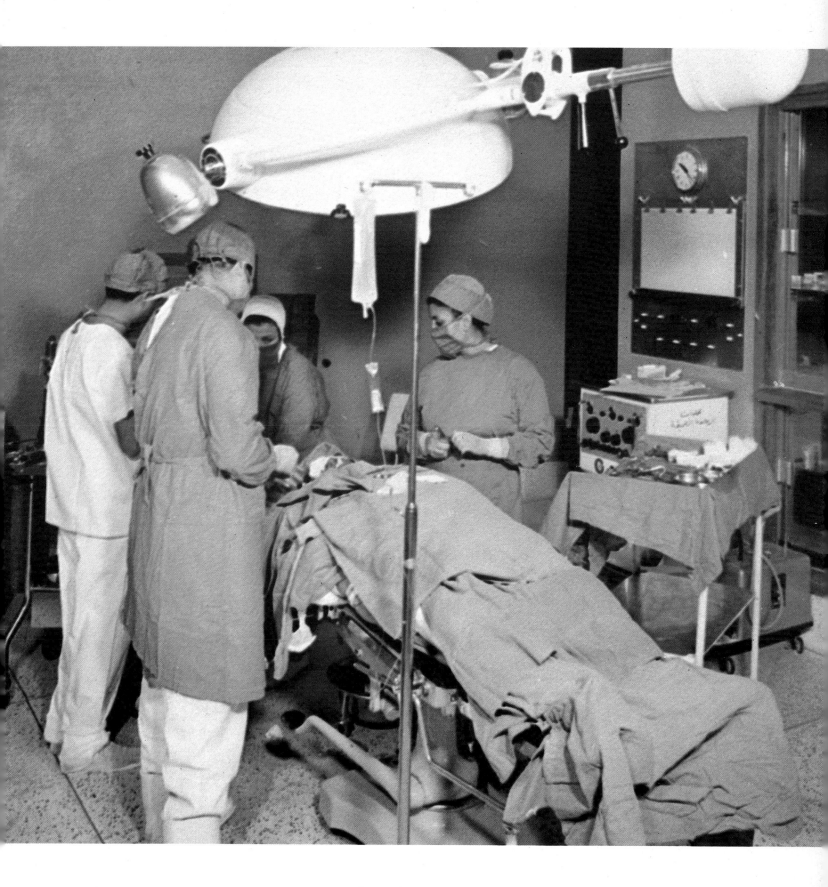

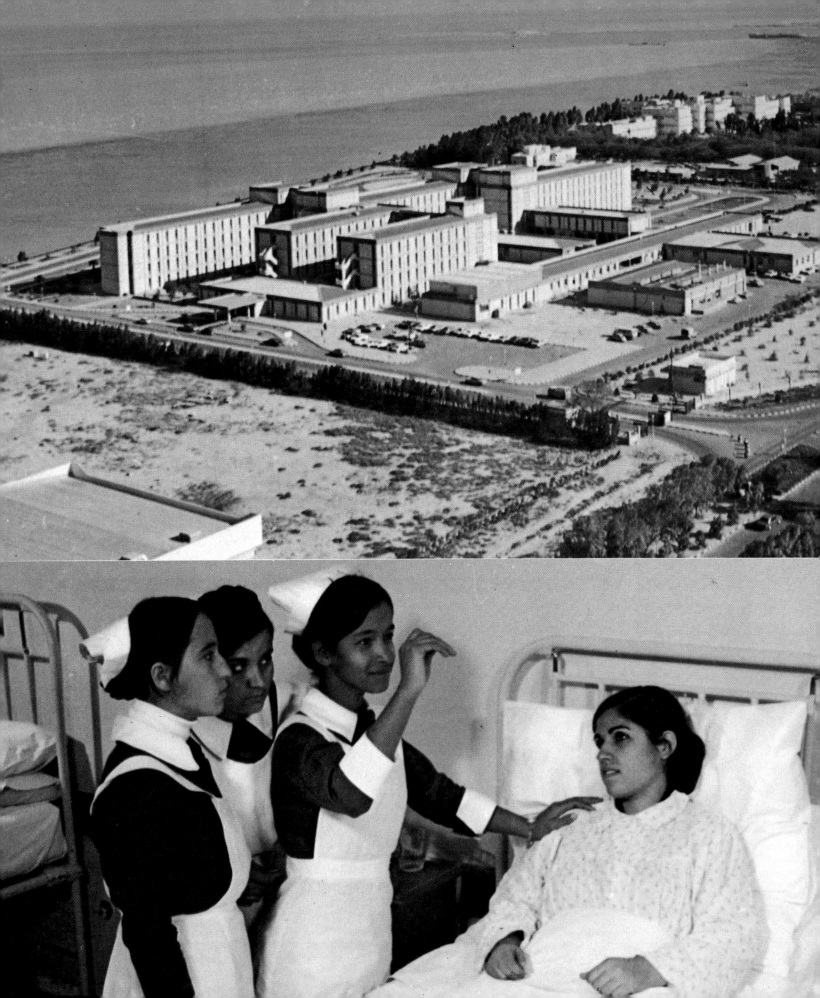

Above left: A maternity hospital approximately 10 kilometres from the centre of Kuwait City.
Below left: A patient at a maternity hospital.
Below right: Students at the Kuwait Nursing School

The Ministry, in addition to its medical facilities, has established wireless stations to provide quick connections between health centres, a large fleet of ambulances, some attached to the fire service, the army and police, and a helicopter available for emergency cases from Failaka Island or far in the desert. Every year extensive programmes have been launched to make the population health-conscious by such means as publications, school lectures, radio and television campaigns. Strict medical supervision is exercised at all points of entry into the State and valid vaccination certificates against smallpox are required. Entrants from cholera areas must carry valid inoculation certificates.

In addition to the rebuilding of the Amiri Hospital Kuwait will also have the Great Mubarak Hospital, with 1,050 beds, and the Fahaheel Hospital, which will serve the Ahmadi area and have a capacity of 500 beds. The Great Mubarak Hospital will comprise two main hospital buildings, each made up of 8 floors and basement, about 14 buildings for out-patients of one or two floors, 8 buildings for services, a mosque and housing for all nurses and intern doctors. The total floor areas of the Fahaheel Hospital buildings will be around 50,000 square metres. There will be out-patients' departments, a hall for lectures, a library and housing for nurses and for intern doctors. These new hospitals will give Kuwait almost 6,000 hospital beds in the public sector and will greatly increase the total of medical personnel to provide one of the highest doctor–patient ratios in the world.

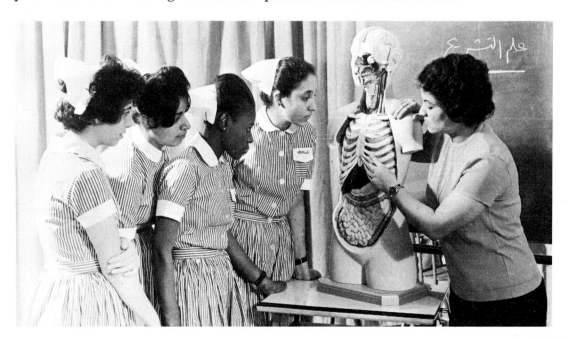

Education

Kuwait's expenditure on education surpasses even that of the public-health sector. There have been enormous leaps since 1949 when the total expenditure was KD. 357,766 (about $1.25 million) and this has been the pattern ever since oil wealth enabled the government to establish the all-embracing social-welfare benefits that have made Kuwait unique. Government expenditures since 1967–68 indicate the importance the government has placed on producing a highly literate population and on increasing year by year the number of educational institutions of all kinds. In 1967–68 education was given KD. 22,250,000. The following year it received KD. 25,276,000 and then up to KD. 27,928,000 in 1969–70. In 1970–71 the figure was KD. 29,911,000. In 1971–72 it reached KD. 35,118,000 and in 1972–73 KD. 45,121,000.

Kuwaitis enjoy free education in all its stages from kindergarten to university. During the entire time spent schooling students are given free text books, exercise books and clothing. Sometimes a generous monetary allowance is provided when there is no able-bodied bread-winner in a family. Attention has also been given to children who require special care such as the mentally retarded, the blind and the deaf and dumb. A large and well-equipped special institute for handicapped children provides both education and vocational training.

A sound education programme is the most urgent need of any growing nation: to run an administration efficiently many thousands of trained employees are needed. In the early years of oil affluence there were few Kuwaitis with the necessary knowledge and background to hold the reins in any department of an expanding administrative machine. Men had to be found to fill posts at all levels, from positions of great responsibility close to the ministers down to the less demanding clerical posts. The raw material was the young Kuwaiti, the youth of the nation. An abundant and increasing supply of highly educated people has become the absolute prerequisite of social and economic development in the world. In Kuwait the country's youth accepted the challenge and the government provided the means for the evolution from an educationally backward past to the highly literate present. Today the highly educated Kuwaiti has become the central resource of the State's society and the credit must go to a government which, with remarkable foresight, planned its priorities wisely from the start of the flow of oil money only about two decades ago.

At first most of Kuwait's professional posts were filled by foreigners. Narrowing the gulf between expatriates and Kuwaitis immediately became a principal objective. Education means Kuwaitisation—Kuwaiti control of Kuwait's natural resources, Kuwaiti direction at the helm of every State function. This goal, in great measure, has now been realised. What gaps have been left on the executive level will soon be closed as the educational programme, the magnitude of which defies per capita comparisons, is still geared to rapid expansion, particularly at the university level.

Schools, of course, came first. They are the foundation on which higher learning is supported. Before 1912, when Kuwait's first modern school was opened, the country had the type of teaching that was common at that time throughout the Middle East. Children visited the home of the teacher. The curriculum did not extend beyond reading, writing and studying the Holy Quran—perhaps with some arithmetic added. The children smeared clay on wood and then wrote on the clay with a stick. Parents paid the teachers about one rupee a month or, if they were poor, gave him a chicken or similar gift. The children left school between the ages of eight and ten and celebrated the occasion by parading through the town collecting money, their reward for learning to read the Holy Quran.

In 1912, a group of merchants pooled resources to open the Mubarekeyah School. The headmaster wrote his own text books and had them copied and some of his teachers were recruited from other Arab countries. The school concentrated mainly on arithmetic and correspondence for at that time the need was for clerks who could keep business records. In the early 1930s some teachers were recruited from Palestine and the syllabus was expanded to include history, geography and drawing. The school was closed down in 1931 because of the economic recession caused by the decline in the pearling industry. The desk of the headmaster, which was used throughout the school's history, is now displayed at Kuwait's Museum of Education.

A new system of education began in 1936 when more teachers arrived from Palestine. In 1937 girls attended school for the first time—140 of them joining 620 boys but in strict segregation. A special tax was levied by the government to finance education and the first council to supervise teaching was founded. From that time on, progress was slow but steady. In 1954, there were 41 schools in Kuwait but 1955 saw the start of what was to become a phenomenal rate of progress. Two Arab educational experts visited Kuwait to make recommendations for a comprehensive educational system and their suggestions were adopted. There are now three stages in a child's education: primary (elementary), intermediate and secondary.

In 1962, the Department of Education became the Ministry of Education and the expansion of facilities began in earnest. In 1948–49, the total number of students in public schools was 4,665. In 1973–74, the total was 169,417. The number of teachers increased during the period from 198 to 12,607. Good progress was also registered in the student rolls at evening classes for adult literacy and education. The number of centres increased from 18 in 1972–73 to 135 the following year. A total of 22,871 students were attending the centres. Total expenditure on public education in 1973–74 amounted to about 17.4 per cent of the total government outlay. Similarly, private education has also recorded a rapid growth in recent years, in response to the needs of the large and varied expatriate community in the country. Thus there were 37,670 students in private schools during 1973–74—an increase of 2.7 per cent over the previous year.

In 1973–74 there were 53 kindergartens in the public sector, 53 primary schools for boys and 47 for girls, 44 intermediate schools for boys and 37 for girls, and 16 secondary schools for boys and 15 for girls. This made a grand total of general education schools of 265. Vocational education was provided at 24 schools. They included a secondary school for girls, commercial, industrial, religious, teacher-training and special-training institutions. The advancement of girls was spectacular—from a system which provided no schooling for females to absolute educational equality with boys. In 1973–74, for example, there were 34,130 girls at various schools compared with a total of 41,369 boys in the primary sector, 23,370 in the intermediate sector compared with 30,016 boys and 11,328 against 12,799 boys in the secondary sector. This gave a ratio of 76,046 girls and 93,371 boys in all public educational institutions including kindergartens, vocational and other centres. In the private sector there were 20,267 boys and 17,303 girls attending 81 schools and institutes—a striking comparison with 1960–61 when only 800 girls attended private schools.

All the school buildings are bright, modern and impressive. Many schools have their own mosques, cinema-cum-theatres, libraries, dormitories, gymnasiums, clinics, spacious classrooms and laboratories, sports stadiums,

Above and right: Part of the extensive educational facilities provided for girls in Kuwait

140

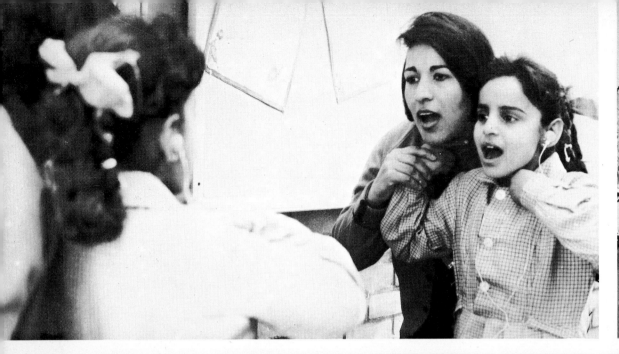

Extreme left: Teaching deaf children at Kuwait's Special Institute for the Handicapped. Left: A kindergarten class in Kuwait. Below: Modern sports facilities are provided for girls in Kuwait

swimming pools and other amenities. There are flats and other types of accommodation for teachers. A huge Nutrition Centre supplies schools meals. The centre is fully automated and all the meals are planned by expert dieticians.

The centrepiece of the State's drive for the attainment of higher skills is the University of Kuwait which opened in 1967 with 400 students leaving school following the 1955 educational programme adopted by the Ministry of Education. As a seat of higher learning today it is unique among its contemporaries because of its continuing majority of female students. In 1973–74, for instance, of a student roll of 3,836 there were 2,249 women compared with 1,596 men. These figures assume much greater significance when it is realised that Kuwait—on the Middle East pattern—is still a male-dominated society.

University enrolment statistics tell the story of the advancement of women in Kuwait: in 1966–67 there were 175 girls and 243 male under-graduates; in 1967–68 girls numbered 407 against 467 males; in 1968–69 the comparison was 628 females and 709 males; in 1969–70 there were 838 girls and 875 males but in 1970–71 the female majority arrived—1,032 compared with 956 males. Since then there has been a preponderance of girl students and there is no sign of the pattern changing. A large number of male students proceed overseas for higher education in several branches of specialised learning—engineering, medicine and the like—and this, in great measure, leaves the local field to the girls who normally remain at home.

While they are still restricted by traditional attitudes the opportunities Kuwait provides for women bear no comparison with the recent past when the veil, a homebound existence and marriage characterised the predominant female roles in society. Oil has nurtured the transition and a younger generation has been raised on the new liberal attitude produced by the massive education facilities offered by the welfare state. For the younger generation of women the transformation from the restrictions of the past to the un-fettered present has been spectacular.

Since it was established the University of Kuwait has become the centre of cultural life in the State, a focal point from which radiates an all-embrac-ing interest in a wide range of cultural pursuits. Prime movers in the spread of such activities have been the members of the teaching staff from far and wide who have, in addition to their academic duties, spread knowledge of the arts, of science, economics, natural history, literature and other topics to

143

obtain the interest of a large section of the population. There are no less than seven libraries within the university, including a well-stocked central library for general research. Smaller specialist libraries for faculty members and the student body are placed close to the various departments of the university. More than 200,000 books are kept in the central library and new additions are continually being made. In addition, copies are kept of all publications made in the State.

The library is equipped with the most modern audio-visual equipment, a micro-film archive and all the equipment required for use with micro-films and micro-fiche. It is possible to record any book or other document on microfilm for permanent storage. There is also the latest apparatus for photo-copying and instant printing. In its effort to encourage the spread of knowledge and to extend the cultural horizon in Kuwait the university has provided books free of charge to each of its students, the idea being to provide sources of reference on various subjects but, more important still, to foster the idea of starting personal libraries. Nearly 40,000 books have been given to students. In other countries it is doubtful if such a system exists but in Kuwait, where the greatest expenditure is lavished on education, it is part of the governmental effort to encourage an erudite society. An average 200,000 people visit the university libraries annually and the books borrowed each year number 100,000. The use of the libraries for reference work increases annually by about 12 per cent.

Looking ahead, the day will come when Kuwait will accommodate more than 20,000 graduates and the numbers will increase year by year. This, in a small population should give a literacy level equal to that of the advanced countries. Indicative of the intellectual output of the university are the courses offered. They include mathematics, physics and chemistry, zoology and botany, geology, Arabic Language, history and geography, sociology, law and Shari's (Islamic Law), education, accountancy and business administration, economic and political science. These are all degree courses leading to M.A. and Ph.D. honours. There are also diploma courses. Total staff in 1973–74 was 366 and this included 10 language instructors, 100 demonstrators, 2 lecturers, 70 readers, 85 associate professors and 87 professors. Of the total student body of 3,836, Kuwaiti nationals made up 52 per cent (1,997). From the Arabian Gulf states there were 742 students (19.3 per cent).

With the object of meeting its future requirements for instructors and professors the university offered 159 fellowships in 1973–74 for doctors'

Above and below right: Classes at the Special Institute for the Handicapped. Below extreme right: An aerial view of the Special Institute for the Handicapped

Left: A kindergarten class working outside. Above: Girl students in the laboratory of a secondary school in Kuwait. Right and below: Art classes in a Kuwait school

Left: Part of the extensive
Library at the University
of Kuwait

degrees at overseas universities. In addition, 488 students were registered for graduate studies in the University of Kuwait. The total of Kuwaiti students on courses abroad in 1973 was 2,228, of which, 1,309 were supported by the Ministry of Education and 159 by the university. Of the remainder 751 were self-supported and 279 were supported by the private sector, notably the oil companies.

The university is now undergoing an extensive process of change. By 1980, the whole campus is expected to be located in the Shuwaikh district of Kuwait City. As a start the entire Arts Faculty has moved into the spacious modern premises of the former Shuwaikh Secondary School, but the Faculty of Science, the Women's Faculty and several other departments still remain scattered. Eventually, the new Shuwaikh site will be a brilliant architectural addition to Kuwait's landscape. More faculties will be created, notably medicine and engineering. Salaries are high and well-qualified teachers have been attracted from all over the Arab world. There is also a vocal National Union of Kuwaiti Students. They have supported such causes as voting rights for women, social and educational reforms and political campaigns.

Kuwaiti students sent overseas—mainly secondary-school leavers—are given generous allowances by the government. Before flying off—mostly to the United States—they receive KD. 30 to KD. 40 as an allowance (now about $150) and an air ticket to their destination. Once in the United States each one is given $375 as the monthly allowance for expenses during a college career. They gather in Washington and the cost of transportation to the various colleges is met by the Kuwaiti Embassy. They are also covered for medical and dental expenses. Every year there is a round-trip ticket to return home, and, finally, a ticket home plus a 500lb baggage allowance. In 1974 there were more than 800 Kuwaiti students in the United States. All engineering students must obtain 70 per cent of maximum marks in the final school examination in order to qualify.

Economy

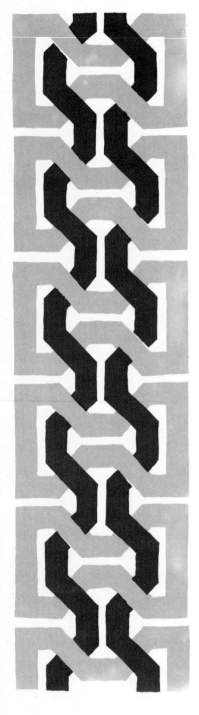

Among the oil-producing nations Kuwait has been recording budget surpluses for more than 20 years and it has been gradually acknowledged in the world's financial centres that the State has evolved a well-planned investment policy. This has taken into account the limited scope for local industrial diversification and the need to build up gilt-edged reserves against the day when the oil wells run dry. While the proven reserves of oil indicate many years of prosperity for Kuwait, it has been wisely realised that these underground resources are exhaustible and that, for the continued well-being of the people, safe-and-sound investments are a prime necessity.

Kuwait's sophisticated handling of its surpluses has earned the State world-wide prominence and the country has become a significant force in international financial markets. In 1974, it was estimated that Kuwait's foreign assets invested in many directions had reached a figure of more than $10 billion. Even before the impact of higher oil prices was felt, Kuwait's public and private income amounted to more than $500 million, about half of which was used for the State and its various institutions. Future portents are that income will grow and that Kuwait must remain a significant force on the international money markets.

Today, Kuwait commands a large amount of liquid assets invested overseas, particularly in London. Its policy has always been to find sound long-term investments and since 1952 it has obtained direct stakes in many real assets not only in the industrialised countries but in other Arab countries and the developing nations. Kuwait's priorities for the utilisation of its surpluses have been clearly enunciated. In 1975, half of the State's revenues were earmarked for investment in the local economy. A quarter was set aside for Arab countries and most of the remainder was intended to assist the developing world. The residue—the floating balance after all commitments had been undertaken—would be invested either in the industrialised nations or used within the domestic economy.

From 1975 to 1980–81 Kuwait's oil revenue is expected to top $10 billion, despite a lower production rate in the oil fields. To this must be added increasing income from investments, greater proceeds from LPG sales and a rising revenue from the processing and national transportation of crude-oil production. Economic experts have predicted a total income of about $60 billion in the five-year period although the actual revenue will be dependent on the vagaries of the international situation and future market trends. The budget for the fiscal year 1974–75 (ending March 31) was set at KD. 959 million (about $3.3 billion). There was an allocation of KD. 385 million to the State General Reserve, part of which would be used for capital participation in mixed-sector companies or loans to private-sector enterprises. This left KD. 574 million (just under $2 billion) for general expenditure. Oil revenues, however, were expected to run at about $9 billion and, after the deduction of grants to the Arab confrontation states (those having territory occupied by Israel), a surplus of from $6 to $7 billion was anticipated.

Kuwait's planners are well aware that there is a limit to the State's ability to absorb a large amount of its petroleum income. At some KD. 180 million the development budget for 1975–76 was about the same as that for 1974–75. With the State's infrastructure and services now well developed the main projects were in the fields of power-generation extensions and new school-building. In addition, KD. 46 million was marked for a sports-leisure complex and a magnificent new mosque. House-construction still proceeds on a large scale and there is a large outlay on defence. Generally, the State's industrial diversification programme has been concentrated on hydrocarbon-based capital-intensive industries. The most important new project will be the building of the LPG plant costing at least $600 million by 1977–78 with probable investment by the government in various derivatives of the industry. Four LPG carriers were on order in 1975 and it was expected that the government would take part in the expansion of the Kuwait Oil Tanker Company.

In 1974, Kuwait was officially estimated to have deployed 71 per cent of its surplus to Arab and other developing countries in aid and investments. These were stated commitments. The Kuwait Fund for Arab Economic Development capital was raised from KD. 200 million to KD. 1,000 million ($3.45 billion) of which KD. 328 million had been paid up. The rate of loan approvals was stepped up and its area of operation was extended from the Arab world to all developing countries. In 1974, loans granted totalled KD. 134.2 million. Elsewhere Kuwait subscribed KD. 30 million to the Arab Fund for Economic and Social Development (AFESD) and about $120 million to the Islamic Development Bank as well as participating in the Arab-

Overleaf: Part of the computer complex of the Kuwaiti government administration

African Oil Assistance Fund, the Arab Bank for African Economic Development (ABAED) and the Organisation of Arab Petroleum Exporting Countries (OAPEC). Kuwait's willingness to use its money to aid Arab countries and the developing world has been shown by its joint ventures with Syria and Sudan among others. Capital has been contributed to OAPEC projects, the Arab Maritime Petroleum Transport Company (AMPTC) and the Arab Shipbuilding and Repair Yard Company (ASRY).

Outside the Arab world Kuwait has provided finance for projects in such countries as Brazil and Yugoslavia. Such ventures are part of the State's policy of direct equity participation in productive ventures and real-estate business. In 1974, Kuwait contributed about $480 million to the International Monetary Fund's oil facility. In previous years, the government, commercial banks and other institutions have subscribed more than $500 million to World Bank bond issues. Early in 1975, Kuwait announced that it would, in principle, support the World Bank in raising loans through new bond issues.

On the regional scene Kuwait's policy has always been to foster close co-operation with fellow Gulf states with the prospect in view of a common market on the lines of the European Economic Community and a unified Arab dinar as an international reserve currency. In 1974, the overriding concern of Kuwait and its fellow Gulf oil-producing states was to protect the Arab world's capital substance and to serve the long-term objectives of Arab development in a world in which the major currencies, badly hit by inflationary trends, lost considerable value and thus caused a reduction in oil revenues. Kuwait, in concert with other Gulf producers, decided to cut the link between the United States dollar and the dinar so far as payments for crude oil were concerned and, through the Organisation of Petroleum Exporting Countries, to reach agreement on ensuring that payments were protected from fluctuations by strengthening OPEC solidarity in the face of market conditions and consumer moves. Kuwait, which took a leading part in OPEC discussions, proposed a collective system of protective financial arrangements for the OPEC states to assist any member state exposed to outside economic pressures because of its implementation of the Organisation's policies and decisions. Kuwait's main aim was to ensure co-operation and co-ordination among OPEC members to maintain balance between the supply and demand for oil in order to limit the possibility of an oil surplus arising, whose offer on world markets might affect the level of prices decided by member states for their natural resources.

153

Economy   The strong position of the Kuwaiti dinar among the world's currencies was reflected by new international bond issues in which the dinar was the sole currency quoted. It was also announced that the capital of the Arab Monetary Fund (AMF), which it was decided to establish early in 1975, would be denominated in a unit of account similar to the International Monetary Fund's special drawing rights (SDR) and known as the Arab dinar. The Arab dinar, it was agreed, would be valued on the basis of a weighted basket of 17 currencies chosen for their importance in international trade. Capital was set at 750 million dinars.

A notable event in 1975 was the establishment, by 10 Kuwaiti real estate and investment firms together with 52 businessmen and investors, of the joint stock company, Kuwait Real Estate Company, capitalised at KD. 3 million ($11.14 million). The purpose of the company is to engage in operations, in Kuwait or abroad, related to prefabricated housing, including the manufacture, construction and sale of such housing and in other related operations. The Kuwait International Investment, which was among the major shareholders of the new company, in 1975 was the lead manager of a ten-year bond issue of KD. 6 million ($20.28 million) arranged for the Spanish motorway construction company, Autopistas de Cataluña y Aragon. The loan was guaranteed by the Spanish government and was placed mainly in Middle East markets.

With large revenues accruing annually Kuwait had one of the highest incomes per head of any country in the world. It was also a large importer of goods and inflationary trends in the world severely affected the cost of living within the State.

The Central Bank report for the financial year ending in March 1974, gave the worth of foreign assets held by government and banks as: Ministry of Finance and Oil, 1,088.99 million (a 15.34 per cent increase over 1972–73) with interest from its investments at KD. 65.06 million; Central Bank overseas holdings, KD. 157.24 million (a 74.4 per cent increase); IMF subscription, KD. 6.98 million (as before); gold, KD. 36.36 million (16.8 per cent increase). Net foreign assets of the commercial banks were worth KD. 389.72 million, a decrease of 5.51 per cent from the previous year. Far higher figures were expected for the year ending March, 1975, as the result of increased oil prices. Investments are handled by the Ministry of Finance (formerly the Ministry of Finance and Oil), the Kuwait Investment Office in London and by various international banks in other financial centres. Major decisions are made by the Investment Department of the Ministry of Finance under government direction. Priorities are: local economy, local production, other Arab economies, non-Arab and especially Moslem developing countries sympathetic to the Arab cause, and international institutions such as the World Bank and the IMF.

In the domestic economy the government introduced food subsidies and government employees' wages and pensions were increased. Budget estimates for 1975–76 put wages and pensions at KD. 247 million, an increase of KD. 60 million over the previous year. A sum of KD. 100 million was authorised for the purchase of land for building purposes. Public works and public-service projects provided for in the 1975–76 estimates (some carried over from the previous year) included funds for new roads, housing, hospitals, a huge sports stadium complex (KD. 100 million), 81 schools to be built over a three-year period, 21 new mosques, new markets, abattoirs, garage expansion works, youth clubs, recreational centres and enlargement of the Hunting and Equestrian Club.

On the industrial front the Kuwait Chemical Fertiliser Company, which achieved a record output of 583,831 tonnes of ammonium sulphate in 1973, continued to increase income from sales. There was little likelihood of the expansion of the industry due to increased world production. It was realised that the establishment of heavy industries faced several serious problems, the lack of labour being the first one. This precluded the founding of labour-intensive industries as these would require the influx of immigrants which would intensify the population imbalance—Kuwaiti-born nationals being in a minority within the total population. Capital-intensive industries were desirable but large-scale viable operations could not be supported by the domestic market and by exports because of their geographical location and intense international competition. Raw materials would have to be imported —except oil and its derivatives—and the end product would not be competitive on an international scale. Thus plans to establish, for example, a steel industry were wisely shelved.

Oil at present makes up more than 93 per cent of Kuwait's exports. Imports during 1973–74 totalled KD. 320.6 million against KD. 271.4 million in 1972–73. Without oil there would be a trade deficit of about KD. 250 million which illustrates the country's dependence on its main asset as an earner of annual surpluses.

Foreign banks are not permitted to operate in Kuwait and the banking sector consists of five large commercial banks, all wholly Kuwaiti-owned, two specialised banks and the Credit and Savings Bank which is fully government-owned. Of the specialised banks the Kuwait Real Estate Bank, established in October 1973 with a capital of KD. 5 million, participates in the financing of real-estate activities. The Industrial Bank of Kuwait with capital of KD. 10 million was established in February, 1974, with the participation of the government, the Central Bank of Kuwait, the Commercial Bank of Kuwait, the Real Estate Bank, the Kuwait insurance companies and a number of local industrial and investment shareholding companies.

Four of the five commercial banks are privately owned while the fifth, the Bank of Kuwait and the Middle East, is 49 per cent government-owned with majority ownership falling under the private sector. Three of the commercial banks have management contact with overseas banks. They are the Bank of Kuwait and the Middle East (the British Bank of the Middle East), the Commercial Bank of Kuwait (Chase Manhattan Bank), Alahli Bank (Credit Lyonnaise). The National Bank of Kuwait and the Gulf Bank recruit management staff on an individual basis. Four of the banks—the exception is the Bank of Kuwait and the Middle East—have a foreign outlet through the United Bank of Kuwait, in which each has a sixth share together with the Kuwait Investment Company (50 per cent government-owned) and the Kuwait Foreign Trading Contracting and Investment Company (80 per cent government).

At the end of 1974, the five commercial banks had 84 branches, including head offices. In the year ending March 1974, the consolidated balance sheet grew by 19 per cent to a total business of KD. 833 million, largely as a result of wage and salary increases in both the government and private sector. Development of the stock market was also a factor. Domestic assets increased at the cost of foreign assets as banks re-examined their investments in some foreign currencies because of the instability prevailing in foreign-exchange markets since June 1971. A higher proportion of the banks' resources, however, was still invested in foreign rather than domestic assets because of the limited absorptive capacity of the domestic economy.

The Central Bank is increasingly fulfilling a central role as supervisor of the system. It controls liquidity ratios and the money supply, supervises exchange positions and calculates and publishes the rate of the dinar against world currencies. Early in 1975 plans were being formulated for the establishment of a Kuwait International Bank as a channel for the government's

Right: The entrance of the National Assembly Building in Kuwait

major investments. London was the likely headquarters and the Kuwait Investment Office there would be absorbed. Branches were proposed in the larger financial centres of the world.

Kuwait is unique in the rapid growth of financial institutions which fulfil the functions of merchant banks, except that they are not permitted to take risks or accept deposits. Their main function is to channel funds from Kuwait and the region into productive enterprises abroad. Apart from specialised funds such as the Arab Fund for Economic and Social Development, which handle government funds, a number of organisations exist in which foreign banks can hold up to 49 per cent of the share-holding if their interest is to the benefit of Kuwait. Among them are the Kuwait Financial Centre with a capital of KD. 3.5 million in which the International Bank of Washington holds shares worth KD. 0.75 million and the Arab Financial Consultants with a capital of KD. 0.5 million in which Arbuthnot Latham (United Kingdom), the Banque de Suez et de l'Union des Mines, the Taiyo-Kobe Bank and Philadelphia International Investment hold 23 per cent.

As Kuwait has expanded, with a proliferation of houses, cars, industries, businesses and increasing exports, insurance business has grown steadily. In 1962 a law was enacted limiting the number of companies to the existing figure. Since then the number has declined so that there are now 3 large Kuwait companies, 6 Arab-owned and 11 others of which 6 are British and 2 American. The total value of the market in insurance premiums which had been KD. 1.5 million in 1962 rose to KD. 10 million in 1972 and to KD. 15 million in 1974. Present capital of the three Kuwaiti insurance companies is KD. 2.75 million with combined reserves of KD. 2.14 million. Although re-insurance is mainly arranged by London, the three Kuwait companies have now formed their own reinsurance company with a capital of KD. 1 million in which 5 banks and 2 investment companies participate.

The Central Bank report for 1974 records a substantial increase in both volume and value of transactions in the Kuwait stock market. Some 10,600,000 shares were recorded, an increase of 283.5 per cent.

Left: The telecommunications satellite at Umm al-Aish which enables the Kuwaiti people to see television programmes from all over the world.

Generous Aid

Kuwait, which for the past 25 years has devoted a massive amount of money to building a twentieth-century showpiece of progress on the desert steppes, has—with remarkable generosity—bestowed a large part of its wealth on the less fortunate developing countries, particularly those in the Arab world. For a small country with a small population Kuwait today has earned for itself the gratitude of many governments and the admiration of a watching world for its selfless disbursement of aid made possible by the rich bounty of oil it possesses as a wholly-owned national asset. By 1975, Kuwait had become by far the world's largest donor in relation to GNP and also the world's biggest provider of aid in terms of per capita averages.

The major distribution agency for Kuwaiti assistance is the Kuwait Fund for Arab Economic Development which in 1974, extended the scope of its operations to cover the entire developing world. In May of that year the KFAED capital was raised from KD. 200 million (about $680 million) to KD. 1,000 million (more than $3,400 million) to give it a potential lending ceiling of $10,000 million based on its capacity to borrow more than twice its capital amount and the addition of reserves. In a letter to the Secretary-General of the United Nations, Kuwait's Permanent Representative at the UN described the fund as the most independent international aid institution ready to extend assistance to any developing country regardless of its ideological and political background. This was in accordance with Kuwait's traditional policy of non-alignment with power blocs, support for an Arab brotherhood in all spheres of endeavour and a genuine desire to use its prosperity on a universal scale to help the under-privileged peoples of the world.

The KFAED was established in 1961 with an original capital of KD. 50 million (about $150 million at the time) which was then a quarter of the annual national income. In 1962, the capital was increased to KD. 200 million and authority was given to mobilise additional resources through borrowing on the international money market up to an amount of twice the capital and reserves with or without the guarantee of the Government of Kuwait. In 1974, the report of the Chairman of the Development Assistance Committee of the Organisation for Economic Co-operation and Development (OECD) offered emphatic testimony to Kuwait's emergence as an international donor of aid:

"Estimated net aid disbursements from Kuwait totalled $154 million (5.4 per cent of GNP) in 1970; $240 million (7.5 per cent of GNP) in 1971; $138 million (3.5 per cent of GNP) in 1972; and $207 million (4.8 per cent of GNP) in 1973. Including World Bank bond purchases, Kuwait's official net flows amounted to between 6 and 10 per cent of GNP in recent years, to which should be added sizeable private investments in a number of developing countries, making Kuwait by far the world's largest donor in relation to GNP. In 1974, commitments to Arab and African countries and subscriptions to multilateral institutions may amount to over $1 billion or more than one-tenth of Kuwait's expected oil income this year. Over 90 per cent of its aid consists of grants, mainly bilateral ones. Kuwait has participated in the four replenishments of IDA's (International Development Association's) resources with an amount of $50 million and has made an advance contribution to the fourth replenishment. It also decided to contribute an amount of $480 million to the International Monetary Fund in connection with the oil facility. Kuwait is the sixth largest purchaser in World Bank bonds. So far there have been six bond issues by the World Bank in Kuwait totalling $401 million . . ."

According to statistics released by OECD in 1974, actual disbursements that year were more than nine per cent of GNP. Breakdowns of OPEC aid by the International Monetary Fund and the UN Conference on Trade and Development for the period from early 1973 until the middle of 1975 show that Kuwait's actual disbursements of $3.25 billion were only $270 million less than those of its much larger neighbour, Saudi Arabia, and higher than those of other member states. The calculations included loans to the International Monetary Fund's oil facility as well as to the World Bank. A striking aspect of the figures is the 78.3 per cent which was extended bilaterally.

In terms of GNP the comparison between the Kuwait aid programme and those of the richest industrialised countries produces a ratio of about 20:1. The effort is all the more praiseworthy when it is realised that Kuwait's only major resource is a stock of depletable oil supplies which are expected—on the basis of actual known reserves and the current rate of extraction—to last an estimated 70 years. In the case of the advanced industrialised countries or the highly developed agricultural nations there is no sole source of income

Generous Aid but a continuing productive and reproductive process which has produced a dependable source of income without limit. Thus, the World Bank has recently advanced a 30 per cent figure to be allowed in the calculation of Kuwait's GNP for the exhaustion of resources. This, of course, is a tentative estimate. If the comparison were to be made in terms of the overall net flow of resources (including commercial loans, investments and other outlays), rather than on official development assistance, Kuwait's performance would be even more striking. The saving rate of the economy for several years has been more than 40 per cent of GNP and a significant portion of it is invested overseas and in the Third World in particular.

Kuwait has always placed emphasis on bilateral aid on concessionary terms and has won many friends as a result. Under this heading there was the sum of US$415 million drawn from the General Reserve in 1975 to fulfil Kuwait's commitment—made at the Rabat summit conference in 1974—to provide Egypt with $170.2 million, Syria with a similar amount, Jordan with US$51 million and the balance going to the Palestine Liberation Organisation, North Yemen and South Yemen, Mauretania and Somaliland. In addition, it is certain that Kuwait made other subventions to Arab countries. In 1974, among other loans made, were one of US$25 million to Bangladesh and another of KD25 million to Brazil.

Since 1973, the value of loans approved by the KFAED has leapt from KD140 million in March of that year to KD301 million in February 1976. Another 40 to 50 are under discussion. During that period about KD27 million was disbursed. It has been estimated that with a paid-up capital of KD350 the net assets must now be more than KD400 million and surplus revenue about KD20 million to be added to the reserves. This makes the KFAED a very significant financial force in the world.

Yet the outgoings of the KFAED, large as they have been, have played only a small part in Kuwait's disbursements during the past years of oil-plenty. No less than 33 loans have been processed and approved since 1973, bringing the total from 38 in that year to 71 since that time. The concentration is on Africa and Asia but there could be significant extensions to Latin America. Shortly, the spacious headquarters of the KFAED in Kuwait will be expanded by the addition of a large multi-storey building. Since 1973, staff has grown by about 40 per cent and the work has increased threefold. There has been close collaboration with the World Bank on several projects such as the Rahad scheme in the Sudan and the Fund joined forces with the Abu Dhabi

Fund, Qatar and Libya in assisting with Egypt's Talkha fertiliser plant. On a Mauretanian project there was collaboration with the Abu Dhabi Fund and the Saudi Arabia Development Fund.

The policy of the KFAED had always been to lend on the basis of a project's economic viability. No maximum rate of interest is laid down and it has ranged from 0.5 per cent to 7 per cent; normally, it is in the 3–4 per cent range.

There are three categories of aid to the developing world: assistance to multilateral development institutions, assistance to regional development organisations and direct bilateral assistance. Kuwait is a regular contributor to the United Nations and its regional agencies, to the United Nations Development Programme, to the UN Fund for Population Activities, to the UN Industrial Development Organisation, to the World Food Programme, to the UN Relief and Works Agency for Palestine Refugees, to the UN HCR and to the UN International Children's Emergency Fund. Total contributions to these UN institutions were estimated at approximately $36 million for 1974.

Outside the KFAED, Kuwait contributed US$480 million to the IMF's oil facility and a further US$120 million for the year 1974–75. Kuwait has subscribed to a volume of World Bank paper which forms part of the bond portfolio of the General Reserve as well as sponsoring IBRD (International Bank for Reconstruction and Development) issues in Kuwaiti dinars worth about US$450 million.

Early in 1976, the National Assembly approved a contribution of US$20 million to the World Bank's "third window" facility as well as US$10 million for the UN Emergency Assistance Fund. During 1974, it gave US$36 million to various UN agencies, including the Relief and Works Agency for Palestinian Refugees. In addition, Kuwait has shares of KD30 million in the capital of the Arab Fund for Economic and Social Development, the equivalent of SDR100 million in the Islamic Development Bank and US$20 million in the Arab Bank for Economic Development in Africa. It has also provided nearly US$50 million for special funds to assist African and non-producing countries to pay their oil bills.

A constant feature of Kuwait's international assistance policy has been its support for the World Bank. Its subscription to the Bank's capital is about $84 million, 10 per cent of which is paid in. International Bank for Reconstruction and Development bond issues in Kuwait have amounted to about $442 million besides the investment of funds in other IBRD issues. This is in

Generous Aid   addition to Kuwait's contribution to IDA replenishments and its participation in the IMF oil facility. It has also actively supported the IBRD move to provide concessionary finance to the developing world on terms half-way between normal IBRD interest rates and those of the IDA.

In terms of regional development Kuwait is one of the major members of the Arab Fund for Economic and Social Development, the creation of which it originally promoted. Kuwait's share of the capital of the Fund is 30 per cent or about $102 million. It is also a member of the Arab Bank for African Economic Development with a $20 million share, in the OAPEC oil facility for Arab non-oil states ($17 million), the Arab-African Oil Assistance Fund designed to meet increased oil prices ($430 million) and in the Islamic Bank established to provide assistance bearing no interest charges ($100 million SDRs). A loan of $17 million was made to the Asian Development Bank in 1974.

The bulk of Kuwait's aid is in the form of direct bilateral loans and grants, mostly through the Kuwait Fund for Arab Economic Development. The Fund's Board of Directors is headed by the Heir Apparent and Prime Minister and comprises eight members from the private sector in order to ensure autonomy and operational flexibility. There is neutrality regarding the political and social ideologies of borrower countries and a constant effort is always made to protect a recipient's interest in contracts or other agreements made as a result of loans. The Fund mainly finances special projects or groups of projects and it does not provide balance of payments or budgetary support. The proceeds of the loans granted are entirely free from any procurement limit and are used, as a rule, on the basis of international competitive bidding.

All the loans made qualify to be known as official development assistance, the so-called grant element in the loans ranging from about 30 per cent to more than 85 per cent. Interest rates are usually 3 per cent or 4 per cent, according to the nature of the project, and include a 1.5 per cent service charge. When the country's situation requires, interest may be waived except for the service charge. Maturities range from about 12 years to 50 years with an adequate grace period during which no repayment of principal and interest is made.

In addition to loans the Fund also provides a number of technical assistance grants-in-aid and services. These generally support techno-economic studies with the object of identifying development opportunities and preparing suitable projects for finance. Building up resources such as banking, power generation and agriculture are major aims of the Fund and, in the sphere of education and training, the Fund actively supports the Arab Planning Institute which is located in Kuwait. Direct inter-government loans credits and grants have also been provided by Kuwait: A prime example is the annual $50 million grant to Egypt, Syria and Jordan as general support. The amounts of such direct government assistance are believed to have reached considerable figures.

The Kuwait Fund for Arab Economic Development was described by Dr. A. K. Ghosh, economic adviser to the Indian Government as an "example of the sympathetic and generous policy followed by the Government of Kuwait for the greater progress and solidarity of the entire Third World". In Kuwait the official view is that the world-wide fund of goodwill that the country's liberality has produced is reward enough for the effort. Internationally, perhaps, the best description of Kuwait's generosity was that of a Western journalist who coined the phrase "Father Christmas of the Middle East" to which must now be added the worlds "and of the Developing World".

Islamic Heritage

One of Kuwait's most important ministries is that of Awqaf and Religious Affairs which, in a cosmopolitan community today, preserves the Islamic heritage of the people and of their fellow Moslems who have become residents in the country since the discovery of oil. The Arabic word *Waqf* (plural: *Awqaf*) means "religious endowment" and denotes a primary function of the Ministry—the control and use of religious funds, endowments and property, the assets of which are to be used for religious purposes. These assets are used for charitable purposes not only in Kuwait but in other parts of the Islamic world. Other appropriations are for the upkeep of mosques and the maintenance of the imans who are the officiating "religious leaders" of the faithful. An academy staffed by learned scholars is maintained to give guidance to preachers and others actively connected with the State's Mosques and to impart a thorough knowledge of the tenets of Islam.

Ministry experts have prepared many publications, including a three-volume encyclopaedia in Arabic dealing with theology, Islamic laws and customs and many other topics. There are more than 300 Mosques in the country and others are under construction. The Ministry's staff numbers 2,500.

One of the greatest pillars of Islam is the act of pilgrimage—to Mecca, the holy city of the faith. Kuwait regularly provides a large number of pilgrims every year and accommodates thousands of Moslems from other countries who use the State as a transit point. This is the time that the Ministry, with other government departments, caters for the well-being of the travellers at Kuwait's unique Pilgrims' City where board and lodging and essential services are provided over the entire period of the Haj (Pilgrimage). Preparation for the Haj start at Ramadhan (The Moslem fasting month which begins just over three months before the pilgrimage). Tents are set up in allocated plots where travel managers exhibit the facilities they offer, arrange lists of pilgrims and finalise the travel formalities. Each vehicle which will take the pilgrims to Mecca must carry documents endorsed by the Saudi Arabian authorities to ensure a smooth border crossing and the Kuwait authorities demand guarantees from the carriers (in the form of a cash deposit) that they will adequately look after the comfort and well being of their passengers.

The number of vehicles in a pilgrimage "caravan" varies greatly but whatever their size they must be accompanied by a first-aid car manned by members of the Kuwait Red Crescent Society. A typical "caravan" consists of a car for the manager, a mobile mechanical workshop and mechanically approved coaches. There are trucks to carry tents, equipment, luggage and food supplies which include rice, vegetables, canned food and sheep to be slaughtered and eaten on the journey. Water tankers, which must accompany the pilgrims are invariably loaded with firewood, huge pots and pans and kettles for cooking and making hot drinks. Major "caravans" are always headed by an Emir of Haj, literally a Prince of Pilgrimage and include doctors, nurses, medical-care units, medicines and ambulances.

The route through Kuwait is to the border post at Nowaisseeb which is reached without delay. There is usually a delay at Zargani 135 kilometres from Kuwait, where scores of vehicles await their turn to be checked for entry into Saudi Arabia. Once these formalities have been observed the journey to Mecca proceeds via Damman, Riyadh and Medina. The pilgrimage begins at Medina, where the buses settle for a week or more. There are daily visits to the tomb of the Holy Prophet Mohammed and vast crowds pray in the Prophet's Mosque. Then the joy of reaching Mecca, the goal of devout Moslems the world over. Here they find the Kuwaiti medical mission ready to serve their needs with the most modern clinical and surgical facilities. Tents are pitched and an intense spiritual excitement permeates the milling crowd. On the ninth day there the pilgrimage is brought to an emotion-filled climax by the Waqfa, or Standing on Arafat. There are prayers on the tenth day and then the long journey home starts.

Every year since 1956, Kuwait's Ministry of Public Health has provided a travelling medical mission to help pilgrims of many nationalities at the holy sites. In 1974, about 8,000 Kuwaitis made the pilgrimage and the medical mission treated more than 30,000 cases. That year the mission comprised 8 doctors, 8 male nurses, 4 female nurses, 2 pharmacists, 5 assistant pharmacists, clerks, cooks and ancillary staff. The mission also includes a religious adviser, a small group from the Ministry of Posts, Telegraphs and Telephones, Ministry of Interior personnel and a team from the Kuwait Broadcasting Services. At Medina and Mecca there are permanent sites where the mission establishes its headquarters. In other areas the members work from tents in close co-operation with Saudi Arabian medical authorities and day and night services are maintained.

Telecommunications

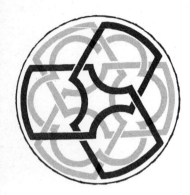

Some 70 kilometres north of Kuwait City a massive antenna structure 35 metres high dominates the flat desert landscape. Around it, dwarfed by the steel dish at the top of the antenna which weighs 350 tons and measures 30 metres in diameter, are a cluster of single-storey buildings. This is Kuwait's Satellite Communication Earth Station at Umm Al-Aish. Inaugurated in 1969, the station today provides Kuwait with instant communication with the wide world outside—a vivid contrast with the historical past when Kuwait's famous "Desert Express" camel caravans carried the mail to Aleppo in about fourteen days. Umm Al-Aish today is the site of heavy hardware: the steel dish is supported by a massive base and heavy engineering works are apparent everywhere. Yet the huge reflector is controlled by some of the most delicate instruments ever constructed and may be moved, effortlessly, through visually imperceptible manoeuvres.

Electric power to run the station now comes from the mains supply. In the early days diesel-engined alternators were used and, with summer sand-storms averaging five a week, maintenance problems were serious. Ancillary services such as lighting and air-conditioning operate directly off the mains supply but on the electronic side the general source of supply is the battery room. Here, banks of 2,000 amp-hour-capacity batteries "float" on charge to supply a steady 216 volts and ensure a stable current flow. This power can then be converted and transformed to meet precisely the requirements of each piece of apparatus. The nerve centre is the control room where one man at the master-control console has the station at his finger-tips. Seated before a massive array of dials, switches, buttons, warning lights and constantly changing digits he can track every detail of the station's functioning. There is a mass of data concerning signals going and coming, circuits in use and available, antenna elevation and azimuth, wind speed and direction, rainfall. He can speak without delay to any other similar station on earth.

In operation, the Umm Al-Aish antenna is trained on a satellite stationed over the Indian Ocean. This satellite, *Intelsat IV Flight 5*, transmits a continuous beacon signal on to which the antenna automatically locks. Occasionally—but this is rare—the antenna might "lose" the satellite but provision against this contingency is made. The satellite's minor wanderings in its orbit are known in advance and the antenna can be manually adjusted from the control room until it is, once again, locked on the beacon signal. This operation takes only a few seconds. The antenna and the satellite remain lined up for the passage of signals coming and going. A transmitted signal with the frequency of 6 gigahertz leaves the feed device—situated at the centre of the main reflector—to be returned by a secondary reflector to the main reflector and thence to the satellite. Signals are received in the reverse of this sequence on a frequency of 4 gigahertz. The present capacity of Umm Al-Aish is 132 channels of which 82 are presently in use. With minor additions the capacity could be increased to 252 channels. Simultaneously with telephone and telegraph operations, 1 TV vision and 2 TV sound channels can be employed.

Owing to the characteristics of the extremely high frequencies used in transmission and reception (which obey laws similar to those governing the behaviour of light rays) the direct range of the satellite is limited to what may be called "line of sight". Thus, within "single-hop" range of Kuwait are: The United Kingdom, France, Germany, Italy, Spain, Lebanon, Bahrain, Pakistan, India and Japan, all of which have earth stations trained on the same satellite. To go beyond these limits a "double-hop" can be made. For example, the station in Spain could relay a signal from Kuwait to the satellite over the Mid-Atlantic—*Intelsat IV Flight 6*—from which it could be re-transmitted to the USA. Other options are open. That particular message could be sent by Spain onward by submarine cable depending on the circumstances prevailing at the time.

Messages going out from Kuwait must first safely reach the station at Umm Al-Aish. A telegram handed in at an outlying post office would be sent by telex to the heart of Kuwait's communications network, the Telecommunications Centre in Kuwait City. Between this downtown building, with its skyscraper tower, and the earth station are three completely independent routes: two microwave radio links and one underground coaxial cable. Upon arrival, the signals—telegraphic or telephonic—are converted to the transmitting frequency, amplified and fed to the proper channel to take them to the satellite and their destinations overseas. Today the station is entirely staffed by Kuwaitis, other Arabs and Indians. There are five shift groups of five men each, a 15-member maintenance group and four senior technicians. In charge are the station manager and his assistant manager.

Overleaf: The Telecommunications Centre in Kuwait City

The station has an excellent record for reliability and stands high in the performance charts maintained by the international satellite communications organisations (COMSAT). In case of serious emergency, the earth station is equipped with two diesel-engined generating sets, each of 750 KVA capacity and each able to keep it in full operation for prolonged periods. The ever-present source of worry is dust, which in an arid area such as Kuwait, presents enormous problems. It penetrates everywhere and, in particular, presents a danger to delicate instruments which are essential to maintain communications. A day-to-day battle has to be waged with vacuum cleaners to keep the buildings and their costly equipment as dust free as possible in an area where, humorists will tell you, dust not only invades the refrigerator but penetrates the eggs inside it.

Kuwait has immediate plans to expand its satellite communication services. Preparations are well ahead for the construction of a second station. The antenna of the new one will bear on the Atlantic satellite and is due to be operational by the end of 1977. Kuwait will then be in direct "single-hop" contact with earth stations over two-thirds of the surface of the globe. In addition, a proposal is being studied at inter-Arab level for a "domestic" satellite to be stationed over Cairo, which would then serve the entire Arab world.

The giant Telecommunications Centre is part of the widespread operations of the Ministry of Posts, Telegraphs and Telephones itself the successor to a series of administrative bodies going back as far as 1775. It was in that year a letter—dated July 15, 1775—from Moore, Latouche and Abraham, a business agency in Bushire, Persia, addressed to their Court of Directors in London was recorded as the first postal despatch from Kuwait. It was carried by camel to Aleppo and it marked the start of the "Desert Express". Kuwait's importance as a secure link in the chain of communications between India and Europe was realised. All Gulf mail eventually reached the port overland and by sea and, until 1779, the camel riders of the "Desert Express" undertook to deliver the mail safely to Aleppo.

They were turbulent times in the region. From 1775–79 the Persians occupied Basra and mail was diverted through Kuwait. When they left in 1779, the East India Company sent the mail from Basra again but difficulties with the Ottomans in 1793 forced the company to return to Kuwait which had remained free of Ottoman domination. In 1795, after negotiations with the Ottomans, the East India Company returned to Basra once more and a

hundred years passed before there was a record of postal services from Kuwait. The establishment of a regular post office in Kuwait was first considered in 1902. Nevertheless, thirteen years were to elapse before the first post office was opened. On February 19, 1904, Kuwait approved a proposal that an assistant surgeon of the Indian Medical Service should, in addition to his normal duties, take charge of a post office in the State.

On August 5, 1904, Colonel S. G. Knox became the first British Political Agent in Kuwait. He brought with him an assistant surgeon and a postal courier. It looked as if the establishment of a post office was near but there were still eleven years to wait. Captain W. H. I. Shakespear, who succeeded Colonel Knox, finally established the first post office on January 21, 1915. Postal business, however, had been transacted in Kuwait between 1909 and 1915. Captain Shakespear reported in a letter that his head clerk carried out all postal duties, including the carrying of mail to and from steamers in the agency's boat. Stamps were sold in rupee values and parcels were received. After the opening of the first post office Indian stamps without overprint were used and their place of origin can only be recognised by the cancellation. It was not until 1920 that the name "Kuwait" appeared on postmarks. Earlier mail bore the title "Koweit" and while official correspondence indicates that the name was changed in 1910, many government departments including the British Foreign Office, used the old form well into the 1950s.

Up to 1924, mails were received and despatched by the British India Steam Navigation Company's ships. In 1927, Colonel J. C. More, a Briton, surveyed and made the first motor track to Basra and thereafter all mails to that port were carried by road. The year 1927 saw the introduction of the Imperial Airways Service between Cairo and Basra and this was later extended to Karachi. In 1932 Imperial Airways began to fly over the Arabian side of the Gulf, via Bahrain and Sharjah, and Kuwait mails were taken by road to join the flights. The main traffic was to and from Bombay and the Gulf ports and by road to and from Basra. From 1933 airmail despatches were made regularly when Kuwait was used as a stop by Imperial Airways on the Karachi route. Kuwait air-mail stamps were issued in 1933 and at that time it was possible to send a letter to Britain by the overland route for three annas, or less than one old British penny. This route was closed during World War II.

During the war the office was kept functioning. Indian stamps were used but, in 1948, the administration was taken over by British General Post Office under the aegis of the Foreign Office in London. In 1948, British stamps

Below: A variety show at Kuwait Telvision

overprinted "Kuwait" and surcharged in Indian rupees and annas were placed on sale. The Kuwait office was then given the status of an independent post office with a head postmaster under whom there were three clerks, three postmen, a telegraph sub-inspector, a telegraph messenger, two linesmen and a packer. In 1950, a second post office was opened in Ahmadi. The oil company had run an independent mail office for some years but in 1950 it became a fully fledged post office operated by the company for the British Postal Agencies. Later, other offices were opened in the State and more sub-offices were built in Kuwait City.

The first step toward the establishment of an independent postal system was taken on February 1, 1958, when stamps containing a portrait of the ruler of the time, Shaikh Abdullah Al Salim Al Sabah, were introduced. New post offices were opened during the year and, in 1961, when Kuwait became a fully independent state, it took over full responsibility for its postal service. A full range of internationally valid stamps were issued in various values of Kuwaiti currency. Kuwait became a member of the Universal Postal Union and its operational standard is widely recognised as being as efficient and reliable as that of the old "Desert Mail" which never failed to make its deliveries in an area of almost incessant turmoil.

Kuwait will shortly have a new General Post Office building and Ministry headquarters to replace the existing premises which have served the community for many years. There are two main post offices—the GPO building near the Sheraton Hotel and the Safat Post Office. All in-coming mail is handled at Safat which, like the GPO, will soon have new premises. Outgoing mail is processed at the GPO and mostly sent by air-mail to destinations all over the world. A 24-hour postal service is maintained at Kuwait's International Airport. On completion of the new buildings some forms of automation will be introduced to handle an ever-increasing flow of mail. The growth of the service is indicated by the fact that in 1958 there were only 2,000 post-office boxes for individual mail. In 1974, there were 10,000 at Safat and these are being increased in number. There is a staff roll of more than 200 at Safat and deliveries cover the entire State.

There are now more than 40 post offices in the State and these are supplied with stamps from a strong-room at the GPO under strict security. As the importance of Kuwait increases on the international scene the work-load has become heavier but, despite the handicaps of a manually operated system, the service is universally recognised as being efficient and speedy.

Recreation

Opposite above left: Boy scouts making the traditional Arabic coffee. Opposite above right: Boy scouts in a cookery class. Scouting is popular in Kuwait. Opposite below: A demonstration of physical exercises in one of Kuwait's sports stadiums

In April 1975, Kuwait was the host nation for the seventeenth Asian Youth Association Football Tournament in which 19 countries took part. Earlier, in 1974, the third Arabian Gulf Football Tournament was also staged in Kuwait. Both these events required internationally approved facilities, not only for the matches to be played on first-class pitches but for the accommodation and care of about 200 visiting sportsmen and officials. This was no problem for Kuwait with its wealth of sporting facilities, including massive stadiums, and some of the most modern hotels in the world. Yet, only a few years ago—in the 1950s—organised sport was practically non-existent in the State outside the oil companies. Football, if it was played at all, could only have been the sort of scratch game found anywhere in the world on the open lot—in the case of Kuwait the sandy expanse of desert that spread in limitless flatness everywhere beyond the small urban build-up of that time.

The contrast provided by today's massive complex of facilities for many kinds of sport is all revealing of the great build-up of resources and the government's active support of all public welfare projects. Association Football (Soccer) reigns supreme in the State and rouses the enthusiasm of the masses, particularly when the national team is involved in regional or wider competitions. The record of success is impressive: outright holders of the Gulf Tournament gold trophy after three consecutive victories; winners of the Malaysian Merdeka tournament, victors over visiting national teams or, in some cases, opponents of equal calibre to such internationally known sides as Bulgaria, Rumania, Yugoslavia and worthy club opposition for Flamenco and Santos of Brazil (even with the redoubtable Pele at his best), as well as such British First Division sides as Wolverhampton Wanderers (a two-all draw in 1975 after holding the lead until the final minutes).

Yet in 1968, the local stadiums of the top league clubs remained monuments of dismal emptiness. There was little interest in the game. The Government stepped in with generous grants of money and the game was established on sound, competitive lines similar to the English and Scottish league's divisional competitions. Since then there has been nothing but success. Today enthusiasm is unbounded and wild in its patriotic fervour. The 1974 season

Recreation

Above: The falcon is used in desert hunting; its main prey is the hubara bird, which is now extremely rare. Right: Gazelles were once prolific in the Kuwaiti desert, but they are now facing extinction

saw eight clubs in the premier division and six in the second. From these teams the national squad is selected. There are also the under-20 teams with their complement of prospective stars and, in the schools, boys from the age of eight are coached in soccer under experienced mentors. Behind them is the Ministry of Social Affairs with constant encouragement and solid financial aid. The Amir has awarded a trophy for annual competition, which has become the local equivalent of the FA Cup Final at Wembley in the excitement it rouses.

All the senior clubs now possess first-class stadiums with facilities for other sports in addition to football: basketball, handball, volley-ball, bowling, tennis and, in the extensive club buildings, gymnastics, karate, judo, table-tennis and other sporting pursuits. There are changing rooms, showers, club-rooms and medical treatment centres containing the latest equipment. All the stadiums are flood-lighted. A National Stadium has been built for major sporting activities, including athletics, and a new one—bigger and more lavishly equipped—is on the way.

All this is in the space of a few years. It was not until 1936 that sports were included in the curricula of the few schools that then existed. The only football tournament at that time was organised by the Kuwait Oil Company and this continued until 1951. In the early 1950s several sports clubs opened and the Kuwait Sports Federation came into being. Considerable aid and encouragement came from the government. Later, the Kuwait Football Federation, the Kuwait Basketball and Volley-ball Federation and Kuwait Athletics and Cycling Federation were founded. This was followed by the creation of the Kuwait Tennis Federation and all the organisations were affiliated with their international controlling bodies. Late in 1957, the Kuwait Olympic Commission was formed and this met for the first time in 1958. In the 1960s there was tremendous progress. Many sports clubs were started and Kuwait gradually earned for itself a place in many international competitions, mostly in the Middle East and Asia. Government aid to the Olympic Commission, which started at about 11,000 rupees in 1958–59 increased to KD. 40,000 (more than $130,000) in 1975.

While organised sports are, relatively, an innovation, the Kuwaitis possess a long historical tradition of such desert activities as hunting, camel and horse-riding, wrestling and the like. The State's dependence on the sea also developed regular competitive swimming events.

Falconry on a much smaller scale than in previous years, is still to be seen outside the urban areas. From time immemorial the man of the desert has been a hunter and ancient Arabic poetry abounds with tales of the chase. Falcons, saluki dogs and even cheetahs have all played their part in providing the hunter with his sport. Today the cheetah is no longer seen and the saluki is rarely used in the hunt. Falconry, however, remains though it is now a costly sport. Falcons, birds of prey, belong to the same family as the hawk, eagle, buzzard and kite. They are swift of wing and, in the wild state, feed on other birds and small mammals. Because of its fearlessness and larger size, the female bird is mostly used by the falconer. Today, the most highly trained specimens may be worth more than a new car. They visit the Arabian peninsula during the colder months of the year and many of them are trapped and trained by men whose families have had a long tradition of handling the birds. Once trained the falcon is ready for hunting but today the game is mostly rabbits or hares, wild pigeons and the particularly prized hubara bird, now becoming exceedingly rare. Falcons were once used to hunt gazelles but these and other mammals formerly common in the desert are now rarely seen. As a result of this and of urbanisation, falconry has suffered a severe decline.

Horsemanship has always been an Arab accomplishment. In Kuwait today this has been revived, after a rapid decline since industrialisation, by wealthy families and those of lesser means who have formed groups to restore the fame of the Arab horse which, like the desert animals, seemed to be threatened with extinction. The Arab horse may be said to be the ancestor of the modern thoroughbred anywhere in the world. In Arabia, alas, the advent of oil and the rapid mechanisation of all forms of transport saw the end of the horse—and to a large extent, the camel—as a means of transport. Arab horses gradually disappeared from the scene and, at one time, one of the few sources of the pure-bred animal was Poland.

Today the story is different. All Arab countries are mindful of the great heritage of the Arab horse. The pure-bred has returned. In Kuwait, there are now several stables containing well-kept animals for racing at the Kuwait Hunting and Equestrian Club and the Ahmadi Governorate Horsemen's Association. Some of the stables, owned by wealthy individuals, contain more than 40 horses. At Ahmadi the stables are owned by working men, usually oilfield employees, and the horses are bought and kept on a co-operative basis. At the Hunting and Equestrian Club, which has many other facilities, there is racing every Thursday in the winter months. At Ahmadi

178

Below: A school orchestra in session. Overleaf: The swimming pool at Kuwait University

meetings are held every Friday. There is no betting as this is forbidden in Islam.

Wide stretches of Kuwait's seafront in 1974 and 1975 resembled battle zones with trenches, huge piles of sand earthworks, bulldozers and armies of men digging here, there and everywhere. This was the "battle" to give Kuwait

one of the most scenic coastlines of any area in the world and its inhabitants a playground for the leisure hours. The government aim is to give Kuwaitis and other sections of the population a wealth of leisure facilities that will keep them at home in the hot summer months—there is a large exodus every year, mostly to Beirut and the European centres—and provide for those unable to join the subscription clubs enough cheap recreational centres to cater for all requirements. Ten beaches are being prepared and there is a grandiose scheme to turn sparsely populated Failaka Island into a leisure complex containing a sports arena, a children's amusement centre, a green-belt region, beach facilities and other recreational areas with motels, bungalows, a shopping precinct and a large administrative block. Other islands will be prepared for fishing and a regular transport service will be provided from Kuwait to carry passengers at economical prices.

Leisure activities will be organised by a new company to be known as the Kuwait Recreation and Tourism Company. The government will have a 40 per cent share and 12 companies in the private sector 60 per cent. New sea clubs are being built along the shoreline and these will join such institutions as the Gazelle Club, the Sea Club, the Messila Beach Hotel complex and others which all have first-class facilities for swimming, fishing, water ski-ing and other pursuits. One of Kuwait's best-known attractions, its Museum, will be accommodated in a brand new block of buildings for which there was an international design competition. There will be five buildings to provide a lecture hall, exhibition hall, a theatre, laboratory and research centre, agricultural and botanical departments, a geology section, an aquarium, a complete reconstruction of the Temple of Artemis found at Failaka, and a special section devoted to Kuwait, its past, present and future.

There are now ten public gardens in Kuwait and these will be extended as the new building works are completed. Kuwait is also well provided with cinemas. The State is one of the few places in the world where the advent of television has not seriously weakened the cinema industry. There has been a steady expansion since 1954 when the first cinema was built and there are now ten with more under construction. The present seating capacity is about 14,000. All the theatres are operated by the Kuwait National Cinema Company and an average of 259 films are shown annually. Most of them are American productions but there are also films from other Arab countries (particularly Egypt), India, Italy, France, Britain, the Soviet Union and Pakistan. In 1974, there were 15 athletic clubs and 2 educational and social

180

clubs. There are 27 societies covering scouting and guiding, the arts, vocational subjects, religion and health.

The State is well equipped with first-class hotels, two of them in the luxury class. There are many restaurants catering for a wide variety of foods and the shopping centres are filled with goods from all over the world. Town planning has been carried out to a carefully conceived plan. It has involved the conversion of the old walled town into a modern city of broad boulevards, impressive public buildings, shopping centres and markets.

Though the State is located in one of the most arid regions in the world the present abundance of water has led to the foundation of embryo agricultural projects. These include the government's experimental farm where scientific methods are being used to provide fruit and vegetables. A hydroponics programme was launched in 1955 and produced its first commercial crop in 1969. Here plants, particularly tomatoes, are grown in a chemical solution. Research is also being carried out in the use of treated sewage and sweet water for irrigation and the possibility of using desalinated sea water to raise a variety of crops. The Kuwait Institute for Scientific Research is concentrating its efforts on using the green cover of the desert to support livestock and of introducing useful vegetation for local needs. In addition, the Institute is experimenting with the building of homes lighted and heated by solar energy and with the use of local raw materials in construction.

Colour television is now an accepted part of Kuwaiti life. Both radio and television have become popular features of the local scene and the State maintains a short-wave radio programme beamed to overseas listeners. There are also medium-wave programmes for overseas listeners with most of the transmission in English. There are also programmes in Urdu and the foreign-language broadcasts will shortly be enlarged to include French, Persian and Hindi. Kuwait's new television and radio headquarters is expected to be completed in 1978 after which the domestic and foreign services will be greatly extended and could in time embrace as many as thirty languages. Television broadcasts include Kuwaiti programmes, other Arabic offerings and films in the English language. Many live and recorded programmes originate in the Kuwaiti studios and television plays an important part in increasing public awareness of topical issues. The satellite tracking station provides live coverage of such events as the Olympic Games, World Cup football and international boxing matches. The local FM radio provides a popular continuous programme of different types of music.

Wildlife

The creation of the oil town of Ahmadi and, more recently, gardens along the coastal strip had a dramatic effect on wildlife in Kuwait. There was more cover for birds and more plants for insects which were able to reproduce in greater numbers. More migrant birds began to break their journeys in Kuwait rather than overflying. The change was dramatic. No less was the realisation, by a host of newcomers from the temperate regions, that the desert—in the Gulf area at least—was not a barren wilderness of sand but the home of myriads of living organisms, an animal and vegetable kingdom which, in widespread variety and seasonal energy, became a wonderland of colour and changing patterns.

Kuwait is on the edge of the north-east Arabian desert. It is an arid region but, unlike the sandy wastes of other desert areas of the world, it provides receptive ground for flora that flourishes on the limitless expanse of flat steppes outside the urban areas: the springtime annuals of the daisy family, the thistle types, vetches, convolvulus and many more. The problem of living in a mainly waterless region has been overcome by the telescoping of life cycles to a few weeks. The plants grow to maturity in the springtime, after the brief rains, and seed copiously. This is nature's fail-safe assurance that the species will continue. The seeds may lie dormant for a long time—even for years—but growth will continue. It has been recorded that seeds that have lain dormant for more than ten years have suddenly taken root. Some species, long considered extinct, emerge dramatically on the desert to reflect nature's extraordinary ability to adapt and survive.

The spring season in Kuwait is very short. It is in springtime that the flowering annuals may be found and that proof is provided, in a panorama of multi-coloured beauty, that the desert is not a barren, sandy waste. The springtime rains fall. There is an awakening of life. The desert blooms for a fleeting period of time. There are the annuals, the perennials and the shrubs. The perennials provide the example of how life can survive under the harshest conditions, to cope with transpiration or the loss of water vapour through the pores of the leaves. The reduction of water-loss is vital to life and the tamarisk tree, for instance, rolls up its leaves to present a twiggy looking leaf. The rolling reduces the surface area of the leaf and water loss is curbed. Another safeguard is the development of felted or hairy surfaces which, on the leaves, provide a form of insulation against the arid atmosphere.

Other specimens form hygroscopic salts, a form of water attraction. The tamarisk secretes calcium carbonate (hygroscopic salt). This attracts any humidity present in the air and a little cloud gathers in the vicinity of the tree. The moist coolness can be felt in any tamarisk grove. This makes the ground under the tamarisk very saline so that only the salt-bush type of plant may be found growing there. Another protective device is prostration. Plants grow close to the ground and survive because they are not buffeted by wind which causes water loss. Their own shadow stops the loss of water by evaporation. Even in the blistering heat of a Kuwaiti summer, when the shade temperature reaches more than 45° Centigrade, the plants have the ability to adapt themselves to the conditions. Thus the cornulaca reduces its leaves to spines to cut down water loss.

Seed dispersal in the desert region is done by wind, water, animals, insects and by plant movements. Anastatica provides the example. In the winter it resembles a ball of dried-up canework. As soon as rain or moisture arrives

Below: The desert locust was once a delicacy but modern agricultural methods have now eliminated the swarming of locusts

this apparently dead wood opens and expands to release seed at the most propitious time. Another species, odontospermum, lies in a dormant, dry button shape and opens in the spring rains to release its seed.

There is a wide variety of grasses and there are many species of plant parasites which exist in other forms of growth. The names of no less than 373 desert flowers have been recorded by the Ahmadi Natural History Group and they have to their credit a new discovery authenticated by the Royal Botanical Gardens of London and Edinburgh.

Unrestricted hunting has reduced the animal life of the desert and several species that were once well known are now extinct. Among them is the ostrich. The last record of the Somali ostrich, once common in the desert, was in 1940. In this case, environmental problems seem to have been the cause of its disappearance and the only evidence now of its former existence is contained in fossilised eggshells. There are still gazelles in the desert but their numbers are few. Many these days are kept in captivity and this has ensured the continuation of the species. Nevertheless, animal life is still varied and unique.

Desert insects include the fly, the mosquito, lice, ticks, roaches, ants, termites, beetles and mantids (predatory insects). These camouflage themselves as leaves, twigs or pebbles. Also found are the scavenging dung beetle, myriads of butterflies, moths and caterpillars. The locust, a pest highly destructive to vegetation, has now been eliminated and the only species found near greenery are harmless and do not swarm. Arachnida (a type of invertebrate) include large sapulgids (scorpion killers), scorpions and spiders. Sapulgids grow to eight inches in length. Scorpions also range up to eight inches and are coloured black, green, yellow, red and off-white. The scorpion's sting is painful and deadly to small children.

Where there are pools small fish may be found together with such amphibians as newts, salamanders, toads and frogs. Reptiles include lizards, snakes and turtles. The dabb, a fat-tailed lizard, lives on the plains and reaches a length of up to $3\frac{1}{2}$ feet. It is vegetarian with toothless jaws and its tail, roasted, is a Bedouin delicacy. The monitor lizard reaches up to 3 feet and it feeds on locusts and other insects. In the sand are found many other types of lizards. The most feared of the snakes is the sand cobra which is slim, sand-coloured and venomous. Vipers abound in sand and rocks but are nocturnal in their habits.

Before they were hunted with all types of guns mammals were numerous.

Below: Bedouins still keep flocks of camels in the Kuwaiti desert, along with their goats and sheep

Gazelles used to roam the plains in hundreds. The oryx has disappeared and the ibex, a species of wild goat, has been decimated. On the desert plains, the ratel, which is like a badger, the fox and the civet cat live in isolation. Deep in the desert and beyond Kuwait's boundaries wolves still prowl but they are few in number. Wherever sheep or goats are herded there is the jackal and there are hares and golden sand rabbits. Small rodents include the jerboa, which resembles a mouse, mice, rats and porcupines. Small hedgehogs are often found among the rocks. Many of these species are rarely seen in Kuwait, which lies on the desert edge.

Kuwait's emergence as an urbanised community has, strangely enough, upset the normal trend apparent elsewhere of bird-life extinction. Today, many more varieties of birds may be seen in Kuwait than in the days before oil industrialisation. Climate and geographical position have always provided the State with many species of birds—some of them sadly depleted by hunting. Now rapid industrialisation and urban development have produced new migratory trends and nearly 320 species or sub-species have been recorded in Kuwait at one time or another.

The appearance of Ahmadi and of the industrial area of Shuwaikh, both of which have large areas of greenery, has made Kuwait a staging place for birds instead of a flyover. Formerly the tree-dwelling birds flew over Kuwait or missed the country entirely. Today they arrive on migration and often stay for a while—like the osprey which once stayed for a week, awaiting its mate; when the other bird arrived both flew off. The birds find their ways to the same places every year, an aptitude that still puzzles the ornithologists.

The rose-ringed parakeet, the only species of parrot seen in the Middle East and Europe, now visits Kuwait. It is a spring and autumn migrant and has been seen also in winter. The parakeet, which is green with a pink beak and a pink ring around the neck, is a short-distance migrant, arriving from the southern end of the Arabian Peninsula on its way to the Levant. Another migrant, the golden oriole, sometimes breeds in the south of England. In the spring these birds pass through on their way to Europe and in the autumn return, probably on their way to East Africa. The collared dove has also been seen. It began to appear in Britain in the 1930s and it has now extended its range of flight to Kuwait to nest in well-wooded areas. Peaks of activity are reached in spring and autumn but at other times it is possible to record many species. There are a large number of winter visitors, a few permanently resident varieties and even summer visitors to the State.

Wildlife   Bird life falls into three sections. In the dry, open country of the desert most species of lark may be found, including the desert lark which spends most of the year in Kuwait and breeds there, nesting before the heat. The coastal areas are frequented by maritime and wading birds, from flamingos down to the little stint which is about the size of a sparrow with long legs and a long beak. Third are the cultivated areas which accommodate tree-dwellers. About 500 flamingos were seen in Kuwait in 1974. They are winter visitors from the Caspian and Black Sea region and they usually stand gracefully in flocks in the sea about 500 yards from the shore. Other coastal birds include herons, some of which are migrants and some of which stay in Kuwait during the winter. Gulls may also be seen in winter. Terns are mostly summer visitors which arrive to breed on the coastal sand, but both birds and eggs have been the victims of over-hunting.

Today there are probably only one or two breeding families of brown-necked ravens left. Several species have been subject to the pressures of pollution and environmental disturbances. The hubara bustard, once the ornithological symbol of the Arabian peninsula, has been hunted practically to extinction. It is rare, indeed, in Kuwait.

The average Kuwaiti garden, however, with its green cover and water sources attracts not only traditional garden birds such as robins, warblers and song thrushes but also species which usually seek other habitats. Breeding species are scarce in Kuwait. House sparrows, whose population is much swollen during periods of migration, are much in evidence and breed. There are breeding colonies of terns and there is evidence of desert and hoopoe larks breeding in the State, as well as the small and threatened population of brown-necked ravens. It is probable that collared doves, white-eared bulbuls, swifts and swallows and, perhaps cream-coloured coursers, together with a few others, breed occasionally, if not regularly, in Kuwait.

Since 1970 when the Ahmadi Natural History Group began to make records, more than 260 species and distinct sub-species have been sighted. About 85 species may be regarded as common (swallow, hoopoe, kestrel and crested lark). Others such as the greater flamingo and crab plover are locally common. Another 40 or so birds are fairly common. They include the rose-ringed parakeet and the pied flycatcher. Uncommon birds such as the peregrine falcon and the moorhen account for another 40 species. There are nearly 60 rare birds, such as the marsh harrier and the redwing, and 40 very rare birds, including the imperial eagle and the ring ouzel.

Appendix 1

Kuwait is situated in the north-west corner of the Arabian Gulf. It is bounded in the east by the Gulf, in the south-west by the Kingdom of Saudi Arabia and in the north and west by the Republic of Iraq. Its location makes it the veritable gateway to the Arabian peninsula. The distance between the extreme points of state boundaries from south to north is about 200 kilometres (124 miles); from west to east along parallel 29°N about 170 kilometres (105 miles). The total length of frontiers is 490 kilometres of which 250 kilometres form the frontier with Saudi Arabia in the south and west. The frontier with Iraq is 240 kilometres in length and there are 195 kilometres along the coastlines.

The weather is determined by Kuwait's position between 28°45″N. and 30°05″N. and between 46°30″E. and 48°30″E. The total area is just under 18,000 square kilometres (7,000 square miles). The earth slopes gently from east to west. The land surface is generally flat with the exception of a few rocky hills ranging in height from 180 to 300 metres above sea level. Shallow depressions are found in the desert. There are several islands of which the largest is Bubiyan located in the north-east corner. To the north of Bubiyan is Warba island. At the entrance to the Bay of Kuwait is Failaka Island and there are two smaller islands, Masken and Oha nearby. There are three small islands, Kobbar, Qarwa and Om Al Naradan near the southern coastline. In the Bay of Kuwait are Korein island and another small island, Om Al Namel.

Kuwait is located in the desert zone and has a continental climate. The heat increases during the summer and brings with it a high degree of relative humidity which decreases in spring (February–April). The temperature reaches its highest in the months of July and August when the maximum often approaches 50° Centigrade. The difference between maximum and minimum temperature increases during the summer. In this season the relative humidity exceeds 90 per cent, particularly in August due to the increased evaporation of water from the Arabian Gulf. Winter is generally pleasant and warm but there is a coolness at night with temperatures sometimes reaching zero Centigrade. The difference between maximum and minimum temperatures is relatively high in winter. The weather becomes milder in spring (February–March) and in autumn (October–November).

Kuwait is affected by winds from the Arabian Gulf. The north wind in winter is cold, being a continuation of the west wind which blows through the Mediterranean bringing with it rain. The south wind blowing from the Indian Ocean raises the relative humidity in summer to a very high degree. In winter, however, it is warm and often carries soft sand. The country is also exposed to the "Al-Samoun", which blows alternatively all through the year in the form of sandstorms originating in the Nejd Desert in the centre of the Arabian peninsula. The dust hangs in the air for long periods and affects the clarity of vision.

Rain is rare although when it falls in the springtime it is usually abundant. The so-called rainy season lasts from November to March. The months from April to October are usually dry but it does rain occasionally during this period. There is great variation in the quantity of rain from year to year. Monthly general averages of Centigrade temperatures usually range from: January, 20 maximum to 1·6 minimum; April, 34·7 to 12; May, 40·5 to 18·2; June, 44·7 to 24·8; July, 46·6 to 26·7; August, 47·8 to 26·3; September, 46·6 to 21·2; October, 40·2 to 17·3; November, 34·1 to 7·4; December, 21·8 to 0·7.

Appendix 2

Ministerial list
for 1976

Heir Apparent and Prime Minister	H. H. Shaikh Jaber Al-Ahmed Al-Jaber Al-Subah
Deputy Prime Minister and Minister of Information	Shaikh Jaber Al-Ali Al-Salim Al-Subah
Minister of Education	Jassem Khalid Daoud Al-Marzook
Minister of Housing	Hamad Mubarak Al-Ayyar
Minister of Public Works	Hamoud Yousuf Al-Nisef
Minister of Social Affairs and Labour	Shaikh Salim Subah Al-Salim Al-Subah
Minister of Interior and Defence	Shaikh Sa'ad Al-Abdulla Al-Salim Al-Subah
Minister of State for Legal and Administrative Affairs	Shaikh Suleiman Do'aj Al-Subah
Minister of Communications	Suleiman Hamoud Zaid Al-Khalid
Minister of Foreign Affairs	Shaikh Subah Al-Ahmed Al-Jaber Al-Subah
Minister of Finance	Abdulrahman Salim Al-Ateeqi
Minister of Public Health	Dr. Abdulrahman Al-Awadhi
Minister of State for Council of Ministers' Affairs	Abdul Aziz Husain
Minister of Justice	Abdulla Ibrahim Al-Mufarrej
Minister of Electricity and Water	Abdulla Yousuf Al-Ghanim
Minister of Oil	Abdul Muttalib Abdul Husain Al-Kazimi
Minister of Commerce and Industry	Abdul-Wahab Yousuf Al-Nafisi
Minister of Planning	Mohammad Yousuf Al-Adsani
Minister of Awqaf and Islamic Affairs	Yousuf Jassim Al-Haji

Appendix 3

Table 1 Foreign trade: Leading suppliers (millions of dollars f.o.b.)

	1973	1974	% change over 1973	1975 (Jan–Aug)
Japan	166·80	279·12	67	256·71
United States	119·28	208·56	74	225·26
West Germany	70·32	159·96	127	139·34
United Kingdom	88·08	140·04	60	127·41
Italy	39·12	65·52	67	84·34
France	45·48	63·96	40	58·33
Netherlands	24·24	37·08	67	84·34
Australia	21·00	35·88	70	*20·91
Switzerland	16·32	26·76	64	20·50
Spain	6·6	25·08	280	51·69
Belgium and Luxembourg	17·52	28·44	64	20·53
OECD Total	648·00	1,142·4	76	1,088·30

* January–May

Source: Organisation for Economic Co-operation and Development.

Table 2 Oil statistics for 1974/1975

		1974	1975	% increase/ decrease over 1974
Crude oil production	barrels	830,579,951	670,918,163	−19·22
	b/d	2,275,562	1,838,132	−19·22
Crude oil processed	barrels	47,642,070	28,547,466	−39·85
	b/d	130,033	78,212	−39·85
Exports				
Crude oil	barrels	736,128,642	594,203,295	−19·28
	b/d	2,016,791	1,627,954	−19·28
Refined products	barrels	40,472,807	21,711,536	−46·36
	b/d	110,884	59,484	−46·35
LPG products	barrels	20,523,306	17,251,833	−15·94
	b/d	56,228	47,265	−15·94
Total exports and local deliveries	barrels	846,644,744	686,469,738	−18·92
	b/d	2,319,575	1,880,739	−18·92

Table 3
Chemical fertilizer exports

| | 1973/74 | | 1974/75 | |
	Tons (thousands)	KD/m	Tons (thousands)	KD/m
Urea	477·9	17·4	524·6	35·1
Liquid ammonia	119·5	3·0	153·1	13·1
Ammonium sulphate	129·9	2·9	95·1	3·7
Total	**727·3**	**23·3**	**722·8**	**51·9**
Ratio to total exports	69·0	69·1	70·7	78·4

Source: Central Bank

Table 4
Aid Disbursements and Commitments*
(millions of dollars)

	1973	1974	1975 (Jan–June)	1973–1975 (June)
Disbursements				
Bilateral	363·03	851·25	1,334·28	2,548·56
Multilateral	167·70	352·00	185·60	705·30
Total	**530·73**	**1,203·25**	**1,519·88**	**3,253·86**
Commitments				
Bilateral	477·58	1,056·81	2,546·89	4,081·28
Multilateral	187·70	942·00	243·00	1,372·70
Total	**665·28**	**1,998·81**	**2,789·89**	**5,453·98**

* Including lending to IMF's oil facility.
Source: IMF and UNCTAD

Index

All references in italics refer to captions to illustrations.

Abdul Aziz Al Sager 104
Abdul-Aziz Ibn Saud 17–18, 21
Abdullah I 13–14
Abdullah II 14
Abdullah III 24–5, 73, 173
Abdulliyah 63
Abdul-Rahman Ibn Faisal Al Saud, Amir 17
Abu Dhabi Fund 162–3
Ahmad, Shaikh 18–21, 24, 58, 60
Ahmadi 24, 62, 63, 66–8, 119, 134, 137, 173, 178, 182, 185; *66, 113*
Ahmadi Governorate 26, 178
Ahmadi Hospital 62, 67, 134
Ahmadi Natural History Group 184, 186
Alahli Bank 156
Al-Ahmadi port *106*
Al Andalus 103
Al Badiah 103
Al Badiah 114
Aleppo 13, 168, 170
Al Funtas 103
Al-Jahara 124
Al Khalifah 12, 13
Al Sabah *see* Sabah Dynasty
Al Sabah Hospital 131; *129, 132, 134*
Al Sabbiyah 103
Al Saud 17
Amarat 12
American Independent Oil Company (Aminoil) 68, 75–6, 99
Amiri Hospital 83, 131, 137
Ancient history 8–11
Anglo-Persian Oil Company *see* British Petroleum
Aniza 12
Arab-African Oil Assistance Fund 153, 164
Arab Bank for African Economic Development (ABAED) 153, 163–4
Arab Financial Consultants 159
Arab Fund for Economic and Social Development (AFESD) 151, 159, 164
Arabian Gulf 8, 10, 13–14, 17, 37, 60, 63, 73, 74, 77, 102, 105, 108–10, 111, 124–5, 144, 153, 172, 182
Arabian Oil Company 73, 75–6
Arabiyeh 103
Arab League 25, 73
Arab Maritime Petroleum Transport Company (AMPTC) 104, 110, 153
Arab Monetary Fund (AMF) 154
Arab Planning Institute 165
Arab Shipbuilding and Repair Yard Company (ASRY) 153
Aratrans Kuwait 109
Arbuthnot Latham (United Kingdom) 159

Architecture 40–4, 58, 123, 149; *43, 53, 54, 79, 116*
Asian Development Bank 164
Astano Shipyard 103
Autopistas de Cataluna y Aragon 154

Bahrah 62
Bahrain 8–11, 12, 13, 60, 100, 109, 124, 169, 172
Banking 155–9
Bank of Kuwait and the Middle East 156
Banque de Suez et de l'Union des Mines 159
Basra 13, 24, 67, 124, 170, 172
Bedouin 14, 36, 184; *184*
Bennett, Dr. Arthur 131
Britain 13–14, 15–17, 18–21, 24, 25, 55, 62, 63, 76, 78, 108–10, 123, 127–8, 169, 172, 174, 180, 185
British Bank of the Middle East 156
British India Steam Navigation Company 172
British Overseas Airways Corporation 125
British Petroleum (BP) 24, 60, 74, 93, 104
Burgan 24, 62, 63, 75, 93, 96

Capital Governorate 26
Central Bank of Kuwait 154, 156–9
Chantier de la Ciotat 104
Chase Manhattan Bank 156
Chisholm, A. H. 60
Civil Aviation Authority 128
Commercial Bank of Kuwait 156
COMSAT 170
Conference on Trade and Development 161
Constitution 25–6
Cox, Peter 62
Cox, Sir Percy 21
Credit and Savings Bank 156
Credit Lyonnaise 156

Dahamshah 12
Dasman Palace 58
'Desert Mail' 13, 168, 170, 173
Dilmun 8–11
Distillation plants 66, 78–82, 85, 88–90; *86, 91*
Doha 84, 91
Dresser (Kuwait) Company 96–9

East India Company 13–14, 21, 170
Education 24, 53, 55, 57, 138–49, 155; *140, 143, 144, 147, 149, 179*
Egypt 60, 162–3, 165, 180
Electricity 78–84, 93

Fahaheel 55, 63, 137
Fahed Al-Salem Mosque *54*
Fahed Al-Salem street *48*
Failaka Island 8–11, 84, 137,

180; *9*
Faisal al Duwish 18
Fishing 13, 18, 111
Flamenco and Santos 174
Flight Training Centre 128
Food and Agricultural Organization 111
Foreign aid 160–5
France 76, 104, 169, 180

General Exportation Company 99
Germany 17, 76, 169
Getty Oil Company 68
Ghosh, Dr. A. K. 165
Great Mubarak Hospital 137
Greek artifacts 9–11
Gulf Bank 156
Gulf Fisheries 111
Gulf Oil Corporation 24, 60, 74, 104
Gulf Research and Development Company 93

Harrison, Dr. Paul 131
Hashemite regime 25
Hawalli Governorate 26, 57
Hawalli well 86–8
Hispanica de Petroleos (HISPANOIL) 73
Holmes, Major Frank 60
Horsemen's Association 178
Housing 57–8, 100–1, 154–5; *116*
Hunting and Equestrian Club 155, 178
Hyundai Shipbuilding and Heavy Industries 108

Ibn Rashid 17
Ikaros 9–11
Ikhwan 18, 21–4
Imperial Airways Service 172
India 8–11, 13–14, 18, 62, 103, 105, 124, 169, 180; *17*
Indian Medical Service 172
Industrial Bank of Kuwait 156
Intelsat IV Flight 5 168–9
Intelsat IV Flight 6 169
International Airport 55, 125–6, 173
International Air Transport Association 125
International Bank for Reconstruction and Development *see* World Bank
International Bank of Washington 159
International Development Association (IDA) 161, 164
International Fisheries 111
International Monetary Fund 153–5, 161, 164
Inzak 10
Iran 60, 62, 76, 108, 110, 124 *see also* Persia
Iraq 13, 14, 18–21, 24, 25, 37, 60, 85, 99, 100, 109, 119, 124
Islam 12, 18, 26, 38, 44, 139, 166–7, 179; *79*
Islamic Development Bank 151, 163–4
Italy 76, 169, 180

Jabir Al Ahmed Al Sabah, Shaikh 108; *30*
Jabir I 14
Jabir II 18
Jahra 18, 36, 82
Japan 55, 76, 103–4, 110, 111, 169
Jarrah 15
Jordan 44, 124, 125, 162, 165

Kazima 124
Kazimah 103; *109*
Khafji 73
Khazal of Muhammerah 58
Knox, Colonel S. G. 172
Kuwait
    ancient history 8–11
    economy of 150–9
    education 24, 53, 55, 57, 138–49, 155; *140, 143, 144, 147, 149, 179*
    energy production 78–84
    foreign aid from 160–5
    government 26–7
    industry 92–102, 155; *98*
    languages 26, 48
    map of 19
    medical care 24, 57, 129–37, 155; *129, 132, 134, 137*
    modern history 12–25; *25*
    oil extraction 60–73, 74–7
    population of 13, 14, 17, 24, 33, 44–8
    pre-oil extraction 33–9; *17, 21, 22, 33, 44*
    recent changes in 40–58
    recreation 174–81; *116, 143, 174, 179*
    shipping 103–14
    telecommunications 168–73; *9, 44, 159, 169*
    transport 53–5, 119–23, 124–8, 178
    water 12, 63–6, 67, 78–82, 85–91, 92–3; *53, 86, 91, 116*
    wildlife 182–6
    women in 36, 53, 140, 143; *140, 143, 147*
Kuwait Aero Club 126–7
Kuwait Airways Corporation 109, 124–8; *129*
Kuwait Aviation Fuelling Company (KAFCO) 73
Kuwait Bay 8, 12, 14, 62, 88, 90, 119; *9, 119*
Kuwait Broadcasting Services 167
Kuwait Cement Company 99, 100
Kuwait Chartering Company 109
Kuwait Chemical Fertiliser Company 93, 96, 101–2, 155
Kuwait City 33–9, 40, 53, 55, 57–8, 63, 88, 119, 131, 149, 168–9, 173; *17, 25, 26, 41, 43, 48, 53, 79, 104, 119, 137, 169*
Kuwait Development Board 113
Kuwait Financial Centre 159
Kuwait Flour Mills Company 101; *98*
Kuwait Foreign Trading,

191

Contracting and Investment Company 76, 156
Kuwait Fund for Arab Economic Development (KFAED) 151, 160, 162–5
Kuwait Hilton *56*
Kuwait Industrial Refinery Maintenance and Engineering Company 99
Kuwait Institute for Scientific Research 181; *53*
Kuwait International Bank 156–9
Kuwait International Exhibitions Company 109
Kuwait International Investment Company 154
Kuwait Investment Company 100, 110, 156
Kuwait Investment Office 154, 159
Kuwait Livestock Transport Company 110
Kuwait Metal Pipe Industries 100
Kuwait National Airways Company 124
Kuwait National Cinema Company 180
Kuwait National Industries Company 100, 101
Kuwait National Petroleum Company (KNPC) 73, 76, 92–3, 96, 99–100, 114; *73*
Kuwait Nursing School *137*
Kuwait Oil Company 24, 60–3, 67, 68, 74–6, 88, 93, 104, 113, 119, 126, 131–4, 177; *66, 106*
Kuwait Oil, Gas and Energy Corporation 76
Kuwait Oil Tanker Company (KOTC) 103–8, 151; *109, 114*
Kuwait Oxygen and Acetylene Company 99
Kuwait Petrochemical Company 76
Kuwait Prefabricated Building Company 100
Kuwait Real Estate Bank 156
Kuwait Real Estate Company 154
Kuwait Recreation and Tourism Company 180
Kuwait Red Crescent Society 167
Kuwait Shell Petroleum Development Company 73
Kuwait Sheraton 173; *119*
Kuwait Shipbuilding and Repairyard Company 114
Kuwait Shipping Company 108–10
Kuwait Supply Company 109
Kuwait Towers *116*

Larissa 10

Magwa 62, 63, 67
Mayet Palace 36
Mecca 166–7
Medical care 24, 57, 129–37, 155; *129, 132, 134, 137*

Medina 167
Mena Abdullah 68, 105
Mena Al-Ahmadi 88, 105
Mena Saud 68
Mergab 79, 82
Messila Beach Hotel 180
Middle East Aircraft Servicing Company 124
Mitsubishi Heavy Industries 104
Modern history 12–25, 33–9, 60–73, 74; *17, 21, 22, 25, 33, 44*
More, Colonel J. C. 21, 172
Mubarak, Shaikh 15–18, 131
Mubarekeyah School 139
Muhammad, Shaikh 14–15
Museum of Education 139
Mylrea, Dr. C. S. G. 131

Naif 36
National Assembly 25, 26–8, 77, 163; *30, 156*
National Bank of Kuwait 156; *53*
National Fisheries 111
National Stadium 177
National Union of Kuwaiti Students 149
Natural gas 75, 77, 78–9, 84, 93; *68*
Nejd 13, 17, 18, 21
Neutral Zone 21, 68, 77
Niebuhr, Carsten 13

Oil
    and energy 78–9, 84
    and finance 150, 153
    development of industry 24, 60–73, 74–7
    importance of 8, 12, 33, 39, 40, 58, 92, 101, 103, 129, 138, 155
    ministry 28, 76, 92
    production 74–7; *63, 73, 93*
    tankers 103–5, 114; *68, 100, 106, 109, 114*
Omar Taher Al Zeil 104
Organisation for Economic Co-operation and Development (OECD) 161
Organisation of Arab Petroleum Exporting Countries (OAPEC) 73, 104, 110, 153, 163
Organisation of Petroleum Exporting Countries (OPEC) 73, 75–6, 153, 161
Ottomans 13–17, 24, 170

Pakistan 10, 109, 124, 169, 180
Palestine Liberation Organisation 162
Pearling 13, 18, 37–9; *33*
Persia 9, 13, 60, 170
    see also Iran
Petrochemical Industries Company 93–6, 101–2, 114
Philadelphia International Investment Company 159
Pilgrim's City 166
Police Traffic Department 53–4
Population 13, 14, 17, 24, 33,

44–8
Ports 55, 93, 103, 108, 113–14; *106, 113; see also under* 'Mena'
Power stations 78–84, 89, 93; *91*
Prime Minister 26–8, 108; *30*

Qassem 25
Qatif 13

Rahad scheme 162
Ras Khafji 105
Recreation 174–81; *116, 143, 174, 179*
Red Fort 18
Refrigeration and Oxygen Factory Company (Kuwait) 100
Rhawdatain 67, 85, 89, 90; *60*
Rhoades, Ralph 62
Richmond, Sir John 25
Royal Botanical Gardens 184

Saba George Shiber 123
Sabah I 12
Sabah II 14
Sabah III 25; *28*
Sabah Dynasty 12–14, 25, 53
Salim, Shaikh 18, 24
Salmieh 119
Sasebo Heavy Industries 103–4
Satellite Communication Earth Station 168
Saudi Arabia 21–4, 25, 60, 68–73, 76, 100, 105, 109, 110, 119, 122, 124, 166–7; *93*
Saudi Arabia Development Fund 163
Seif Palace 15; *30, 46*
Seleucid empire 9–10
Shakespear, Captain W. H. I. 172
Shamiyah 86; *54*
Shamiyah Gate *44*
Shatt Al Arab 37, 63, 67, 85, 88
Shipbuilding 18, 37; *21*
Shipping 103–14
Shuaiba 63, 66, 73, 78–9, 83, 89–90, 92–6, 100, 111, 113–14; *73*
Shuaiba Area Authority 92–3, 114
Shuaiba Industrial Development Board 92
Shuwaikh 55, 63, 78–9, 82–4,

88–9, 100–1, 103, 113–14, 122, 131, 149, 185; *86, 91, 98*
Sleibiyah 63
Southwell Hospital *see* Ahmadi Hospital
Southwell, Sir Philip 62–3
Spain 73, 103, 108, 154, 169
Special Drawing Rights (SDR) 154
Special Institute for the Handicapped *143, 144*
Sport 174–8
Sultan bin Mahmoud 88
Syria 9, 100, 124, 153, 162, 165

Taiyo-Kobe Bank 159
Telecommunications Centre 169–70; *48, 169*
Temple of Artemis 180
Transport 53–5, 119–23, 124–8, 178
Tylos 10

Umm Al-Aish 168–9; *159*
United Arab Shipping Company 108–10
United Bank of Kuwait 156
United Fisheries of Kuwait 92, 99, 111, 114
United Nations 25, 111, 160, 161, 163
United States of America 60, 76, 108, 110, 111, 127–8, 149, 153, 169
Universal Postal Union 173
University of Kuwait 53, 143–9; *116, 149, 179*
Upper Clyde Yard 108
Uqair 18–21
Ur 11

Wadi al'Aujah 21
Wafra 68
Wahhabis 13–14, 18, 21
Wallace Shipping 109
Warah 124
Warbah 103
Water 12, 63–6, 67, 78–82, 85–91, 92, 93; *53, 86, 91, 116*
Wildlife 182–6
World Bank 153, 155, 161–4

Zargani 167
Zubair 13, 14

Acknowledgements

The publishers are grateful to the Kuwaiti Ministry of Information for supplying most of the photographs in this book, and would also like to thank the following:
Bruce Coleman Ltd: 32 (photog. C. Osborne), 176 top (photog. N. Myers), 176 bottom (photog. L.R. Dawson), 183 (photog. S.C. Bisserot), 185 (photog. J.A. Burton); Kuwait Airline Corporation: 126; Kuwait Oil Tanker Company: 109, 115; Middle East Economic Digest (MEED): 34–5, 46, 47, 61, 66–7, 67 top, 87 bottom, 100, 106–7, 137, 142 top right; Royal Geographical Society: 13, 14–15, 16 top, 16 bottom right, 16 bottom left, 21, 22, 23 top, 23 bottom, 24, 42, 48, 86, 104.